Your Decisions Determine Your DESTINY

A True and Inspiring Story

STEVEN D. MIDDLETON

Your Decisions Determine Your Destiny

Copyright © 2018 Steven D. Middleton

All rights reserved. No part of this book may be used or reproduced by any means, graphic, electronic, or mechanical, including photocopying, recording, taping or by any information storage retrieval system without the written permission of the author except in the case of brief quotations embodied in critical articles and reviews.

ISBN 978-1-945169-19-9

Orison Publishers, Inc.
PO Box 188
Grantham, PA 17027
717-731-1405
www.OrisonPublishers.com
Publish your book now, marsha@orisonpublishers.com

Introduction

A lot of decisions we make that set the course for our lives usually can be best understood and appreciated in hindsight. It seems only after experiencing the results of our decisions, deeper insight, and more clarity is revealed. I have reached the conclusion that the majority of my decisions throughout my life so far, were not made from the best positional base. For example; Many times, I made decisions from impulse, fear, internal and external pressure, desperation, low self-esteem, hormones, and the list goes on. I seldom stopped and carefully considered my options before making a decision. I never realized until after growing up (which took many years), that your best decisions should be based on good information, and that the quality of life that I would have, is usually determined by the results of those decisions that I would make. Choices and decisions are similar, but not quite the same. Choices are an act of selecting or making a decision when faced with two or more possibilities. A decision on the other hand is a conclusion or resolution reached after consideration. A decision can be an analytical method to eliminate options. It is a thoughtful, thorough process. It is a direction you choose after beginning with choices and opportunities, considering your past experiences. For example, after thorough and careful consideration from our many choices, my wife and I have decided to vacation in Jamaica this year.

There is no doubt that each and every one of us has our own unique story to tell, based on our decisions. While some of us may have lived a quiet and uneventful life, others may have decided to take a more exciting, dangerous, and unbelievable course down the corridors of life. I am one of those individuals. The longer you live, more is revealed about you and your role on this big stage called life. You begin to realize that a lot of experiences you have encountered along the way, good and bad, were not necessarily for you. Perhaps used as developmental stages so that when the time is right, you can be a true blessing to others. In other words, what you are doing in the now has little to do with the present, but instead is actually creating a destination that will unfold for you or perhaps for someone else down the road.

As I invite you to travel back with me through the portals of my life, I would like to take this time to thank Almighty God for keeping me alive to tell my story. As you will discover on several occasions, had it not been for the grace of God, I would be dead and gone. As I began to revisit the various episodes and events in my life, I was amused, thrilled, terrified, and truly blessed. "I come to realize that when you are facing a giant (in any form), it's only because he is blocking the gate...just imagine what's on the other side." Some of the decisions I've made in my life will have you sitting on the edge of your seat, because anytime you make a decision out of sheer desperation, anything can happen to you.

After a while, the age-old question comes to mind, why am I here? What purpose was my life actually designed to function in? When you start to get some considerable age on you, you begin to realize that you have more time behind you than you do in front of you. To say the least, at this time in your life your decisions are more critical than ever. You may develop a sense of urgency in not only being at peace with where you're at, but also determining your very own distinctive role in life's greater design and making the decision to follow that path. Once you decide that you're in, you start searching for clues by doing a personal examination of your gifts, your assets, and your strengths. You also begin to humbly acknowledge your shortcomings and with some help begin to move away from them. Now you're ready to begin passionately expressing your unique talent and finally find your personal pathway towards your destiny. Checkmate! What is your decision?

Table of Contents

Introduction iii

Chapter 1 Cherry Hill 1

Chapter 2 Summer Tours 7

Chapter 3 Harlem Avenue 13

Chapter 4 So Many Choices 21

Chapter 5 US Army 31

Chapter 6 At the Top of the World 39

Chapter 7 Adventures Unimagined 45

Chapter 8 Let's Make Some Trouble 53

Chapter 9 Land of the Midnight Sun 59

Chapter 10 From the Icebox to the Oven 65

Chapter 11	Back to Reality	73
Chapter 12	Where to From Here	79
Chapter 13	A Chance of a Lifetime	85
Chapter 14	I Just Didn't Know	95
Chapter 15	A Different Type of Wilderness	99
Chapter 16	Joining Up With Danger	107
Chapter 17	A Decision for Suicide	113
Chapter 18	Downhill Fast	121
Chapter 19	Baltimore City Jail	127
Chapter 20	Time to Settle In	133
Chapter 21	Back Up Town	141
Chapter 22	Finally, Redemption	149
Chapter 23	A Whole New Life	157
Chapter 24	Mamma Never Been So Proud	165
Chapter 25	Angel in Disguise	175
Chapter 26	Knocked Down, But Not Ou	183
Chapter 27	How Bad Do You Want It	191
Conclusion		201

CHAPTER 1

Cherry Hill

I grew up on the south side of Baltimore in a projects section called Cherry Hill, that was predominantly African-American, a community of low-income housing with the appearance of its own little town. This section of Baltimore would prove to be the leaping point for a multitude of Black families before moving uptown to either East or West Baltimore and leaving the projects behind. The backdrop was the mid 1950s moving into the early 1960s in a time that obviously predated the electronic age. I was the youngest of four and had a strong desire to connect with my friends and play vigorously, as much as possible.

Now from my perspective, it seemed like everyone in my family was doing their own thing, which by the way wasn't just exclusive to my family, but an obvious cultural expression African-Americans displayed, at the time. It really didn't seem odd to me that no one in the family had any time for me, the youngest. Instead of feeling rejected or alienated, I felt free to explore my environment in my own way. I didn't think much of it as I just rolled with the flow. This

YOUR DECISIONS DETERMINE YOUR DESTINY

led me to become creative and innovative in ways that allowed me to cultivate my potential.

During this time, the incentive to build things seemed to be the order of the day. Although one of the toys we received regularly at Christmas was a pair of skates, we eagerly and enthusiastically began to build wagons and skateboards from raw materials. I truly believed that I could build almost anything I attempted. Not exactly sure where that self-confidence came from, but I don't remember anyone telling me that I couldn't be creative. The skateboards we used were designed with a piece of 2 x 4 wood slack, one skate separated in half and attached to each end of the wood. We also drilled a hole 6 inches from the front to attach a long screw, a spring, and a stopper for a simulated brake. Many people at that time didn't have an automobile in the family, and so the wagons became a means of hauling groceries from the store. This practice also allowed some of us to earn some money hauling other people's groceries from the store to their home.

It seemed like everybody I knew owned a pair of skates. We skated all over the section of Cherry Hill; to include the schoolyards where we staged various competitions for jumping over 55 gallon drums lying on their sides and clearing a 14 to 16 foot concrete stairway. A competitive spirit was developed in me at an early age. If that wasn't dangerous enough, some of us would hang on the back of the city transit bus for a thrilling ride while on skates. Frequently, some would stand on the back bumper of the transit bus and hold on to an advertising sign attached to the rear of the bus.

I realized that my decisions early on were usually based on what everybody else was doing. What I was thinking at the time was, "If they can do it, I can do it, perhaps even better." Wintertime was also a lot of thrill seeking fun. We would seek out the top of certain hills with our sleds and build a fly off ramp to add to the excitement.

While in elementary school, we played with marbles, small Army figures, train sets, car racing sets, and a lot of other things that my dear late parents Carroll and Mary Middleton provided. If we were poor, I certainly didn't know. Probably because there wasn't any upper class examples, anywhere near to compare.

Cherry Hill

With the absence of the electronic toys that were to come later, it seemed to force us to play and interact with an intensity that was necessary at that time. We had one black and white television set and at times, the family would gather around and watch some shows. With that building and creative climate that was going on, I decided to get some wood, saw, a hammer and nails, and build myself a little lounge chair. It wasn't soft and comfy, but I was very proud of my design. As I played hard with my friends, I kind of felt a little sorry for my one and only dear sister, Vonnie. Being as she was the only girl, I realized that my mother felt it necessary to keep a tight rein on her. She also was expected to learn how to cook and clean while my brothers and I obviously were exempt. I think that is why she got a lot of satisfaction out of *snitching* on me when I would do something bad, which I often did. Perhaps at least she could feel some sense of justice and satisfaction, if you know what I mean. My middle brother Carroll, who we call *Poochie,* was five years older than I. Obviously we had little in common coming up and my oldest brother Gene, who was 10 years older than myself, moved out of the house in his late teens so he could experience his own kind of life.

I learned how to swim and loved it very much. I was taught how to swim by this big girl that was in the public pool. I was at first walking on the bottom of the pool (around four feet deep), and moving my arms on top of the water as if I was swimming. (Fronting). She then said, "Do you want to learn how to swim?"

I replied, "Sure," and that's how I learned how to swim. I had no clue who she was, however, I was glad that I made the decision to let her help me. I enjoyed track and field in school and won a medal or two as a result. I thought at one time that I could run as fast as Jesse Owens could. As most little boys would do, we jumped fences, flipped over fences, and jumped off the roofs of two-story project homes, landing on the grass of course. One of our regular delights as kids was going to the movies at the Cherry Hill Shopping Center at least three times a month. The admission fee was $.35 back in the early sixties. One of our favorite movie stars was **Steve Reeves** known as Hercules. We used to get so excited watching the strongman defeat his enemies and when we

YOUR DECISIONS DETERMINE YOUR DESTINY

came out of the movies; each one of us was Hercules. Little did I know that this particular screen image would lock itself into my subconscious and manifest itself many years down the road.

Going to the fifth grade I would bring a spool of thread to school with me, and my buddies and I would go in the restroom and see which one of us could actually break a number of threads wrapped around our little relaxed biceps, and then make a muscle to snap them as Hercules did with metal bands. Although I was thin, I was very competitive at a young age. Back then, all gas stations were true service stations. Me and a friend of mine named Walter would sneak off a couple of tire rims in the back of the station, find a pole that could fit through the holes of the rims and then take some wire to secure the rims on a pole and that was our barbell. Only one problem, we couldn't lift it because it was just too heavy for our thin frames, but we sure tried.

We played hard as kids, which also resulted in me getting my forehead busted open twice. I received six stitches both times that are slightly visible even to this day. The first one I did myself by running into a metal clothesline pole. The second time a kid by the name of Raymond Crank, threw a short pipe in my direction intended for a chubby kid we called Turkey, who was agitating Raymond's sister, Diane. The pipe hit me dead on my forehead and cracked it open. There was so much blood running down my face, I thought I was going to die or something. I went home to my mother and she rushed me, once again in an ambulance to the hospital. The nurse said to me before they stitched me up, "You're not going to cry on me are you, because you are a big boy, right?" When she stopped the bleeding and I saw how pretty she was, I fought those tears off. Sometimes certain decisions can become easy with the right motivation.

This was the time for me to initiate some bad habits as well. My very first cigarette tryout was at the age of 10. A younger friend of mine, Terry White, who lived across the street, could blow smoke through his nose and I thought that was the coolest thing that I had ever seen. So I go and sneak one of Daddy Carroll's *Camel* cigarettes and that thing was so strong that it almost made me sick. I was unable to blow smoke out of

Cherry Hill

my nose right away, but I certainly tried. That decision to try out smoking would develop a habit that would span across a 33-year period. A habit that I thought I would never be able to let go.

Another bad decision at that tender age led me to sniffing airplane model glue. Why? Because my buddies were doing it and I certainly didn't want them to think I was *chicken*. Although my friends and I didn't do it often, it was my first experience of getting *high*, launching a destructive path where I couldn't have possibly imagined what awaited me. Things were naturally cheap at that time and I remember one Christmas I decided to get a Christmas gift for my mother and father and my oldest brother. All I had was a dollar and I decided to get each of them a pack of cigarettes, which only cost $.30 apiece, and I had $.10 change, this time was still around the year of 1963.

I realized that I was naturally shy and this was revealed to me when I went to school. Although I didn't have a problem proving that my little biceps were just as strong as my friend's were, if not stronger, however, in the classroom was a different thing altogether. My greatest fear was being called up to the chalkboard in front of the entire class. I was petrified. The fear and anxiety would paralyze me so much that instead of writing something on the board, all I could do was stand there and scratch under my armpits. The teacher would get a little frustrated and eventually say, "Boy, go take your seat." It had to be quite funny. A far cry from the demeanor that I compose when I'm speaking to large groups of people today.

My mother administered the discipline, (which I needed a lot of), because that just wasn't Daddy Carroll's thing. As a result, I began to develop resentment against authority because in my young mind that wasn't the natural order of things. That's not what I saw on television with the *Leave it to Beaver* illusion. The social climate of the 1960's didn't help much either. I spent a lot of summers out in the county with my relatives. My cousin Byron and I were together almost like brothers, we were so close. Those first 12 years of my life I believe was very adventurous and exciting as well.

When we finally left the projects of Cherry Hill and moved uptown, as so many families eventually do, I believe I was ready to enter the

YOUR DECISIONS DETERMINE YOUR DESTINY

next phase of my life. Not really knowing what to expect, being a young skinny, timid kind of guy, I found out that change can be gradual or instant. With or without my decision, change is not only inevitable but also unavoidable.

CHAPTER 2
Summer Tours

Quite often during the summertime, kids are sent to stay with the grandparents or cousins for the summer. Was it a break for the kid, or really a break for the parents? I'm not absolutely certain about this, but to me, I seriously believe that I was the only one to be dispatched somewhere almost every summer. Actually, I was glad to get away for a while into a different environment. Now don't get me wrong, I had a lot of fun particularly hooking up with my first cousin Byron. We were just two years apart and we actually grew up together. We toured my house, his mother's house, his father's house, our grandparent's house, our uncle's house, and some of our cousin's houses. We did what we always did, got into mischief when the opportunity presented itself.

He and I took the opportunity, (around the ages of 10 and 12), to explore the mysteries of the opposite sex. I have to admit, him being younger than I was, he appeared to be a little more comfortable with this *rite of passage* than I was. My shyness was apparent to me at a very young age. We were both sent out to Anne Arundel County where a bunch of our relatives lived in a small town called *Pumphrey*. Now

YOUR DECISIONS DETERMINE YOUR DESTINY

this town was completely different from the row house city life we were accustomed to. To me, it was like being out in the country around what us *city folk* classified as *country folk*. Houses not connected together, no sidewalks on the road or streets and a river in back of the houses. At any given time during our summer stay, we could stay at Uncle J.P.'s house, Uncle Julius's house, Aunt Pecolia's house, or Grandma's house.

One warm summer afternoon after doing a little scheming, Byron and I made the decision to sneak these two local girls down into Grandma's partially finished basement. They were very willing. The basement was half dug out, basically for a small area for Grandma's old-fashioned style washing machine and of course the wood furnace. There were two entrances to the cellar. A pantry upstairs adjacent to the bathroom had a long trapdoor that you pulled up from the floor with a cord, which gave you access to a narrow, steep, wooden staircase and a small door entrance from the outside. As we entered the basement, there wasn't no sitting or lying down, especially with the cute dresses the girls had on, so we stood up against the wall.

To be honest, at first I didn't have a clue as to what I was doing. I felt like a fish out of water. Unlike my cousin at 10, who seemed to be very adept at this new experience. The girl I was with had to give me some instructions, otherwise, it wouldn't have happened. Afterwards, I felt a little weird because my shyness plagued me throughout the entire, brief encounter. At that moment, I wasn't exactly sure what I was feeling. Was I supposed to be feeling proud or strangely weird? Byron and I remained very close and best first cousins all the way up into his recent passing at the age of 60 years old. Perhaps I looked at him as the younger brother that I've never had.

As we grew up and got older, we always knew we could count on one another to *watch our back* whatever the circumstances were. There was one particular incident when he and his family were living up in Edmondson Village, perhaps a fifteen-minute walk from our house in West Baltimore. One of his *supposed to be buddies* went into his mother's pocketbook and took some money out of it when they were in the house. The boy not only denied the theft, but also went and got a couple of his buddies to stand against Byron. He called me up and I shot up there right away. I was never a tough kind of a guy, but he and I were very close.

Summer Tours

So with Byron, Byron's younger brother Kevin, and I, we were ready to battle until they pulled back from us and left the area. Byron has also showed up for me in times of need. As I indicated earlier, we were *best* first cousins from day one. Even him, my wife, and his wife Gloria, loved each other dearly. I miss him so much.

One summer my sister Yvonne and I visited our cousins in Camden, New Jersey. I call these trips *Summer Tours* but for real, Mamma needed a much-needed break. This was our one and only summer away together, just her and I. I remember leaving behind my little sweetheart, Sylvia, who lived across the street. I think that was my very first time my little heart began to ache missing a girlfriend. I was around 13 years old. I honestly didn't get a chance to explore some of the *deeper wonders* with this girl, probably because I was somewhat afraid of her. Nevertheless, I had a sure enough thing for her. I heard a record when I was away sung by an artist by the name of **Linda Jones** named *Hypnotize*, it had my little heart aching for this girl.

Up in Camden, my cousin Andy and I had a lot of fun. Andy was a curly headed kid that seemed to have no problems taking risks. Nothing real heavy, just regular mischief just like yours truly. My sister and I were delayed in returning to Baltimore; on account of this one kid that Andy and I decided to give chase. I can't quite remember exactly why we were chasing him; I just followed Andy's lead. The kid fell on a pipe that was sticking up out of the ground that was positioned as a little wire fence around these people's small front yard, and cut his neck. It was a deep gash in his neck, which had me afraid; I never saw a cut like that before. My boy Andy didn't appear too concerned the way that I was. Vonnie and I could not leave for Baltimore because we had to go to a hearing before we could return. When we entered the courtroom and went before the judge, I didn't know what to expect. It turned out not to be that big of a deal but they had me a little worried. I guess they needed us to <u>appear</u> to be accountable.

During this time, African-American men were undergoing a radical hairstyle change. My older cousin Bill up in Camden, Andy's big brother, who was around my brother Poochie's age, was using a product on his hair that was called *Johnson's Hair Straightener*. It was a glass jar of a white

YOUR DECISIONS DETERMINE YOUR DESTINY

substance, similar to a strong hair relaxer. One of the main ingredients of this mixture had to be lye. What it did for you was gave you what was known as a *process*. My cousin Bill was wearing that style as if he was one of the *Temptations*. At 13, I thought it was the coolest thing ever. When my sister and I returned to Baltimore, I immediately went to the *Reads* drugstore and purchased a jar. I came back home and used the faucet and sink in the basement. We were still living in the first house we moved into on Harlem Avenue, which was at 2723. We would soon leave that house and reside a couple of doors down at 2719 for approximately 20 years. I then proceeded to go down to the basement and applied this hair straightener to my hair. It wasn't supposed to stay in your hair no longer than about five minutes. After that you feel like you're entire head was on fire. And if that wasn't enough, then it turns your hair completely red. You would have to dye your hair back to black. After subjecting myself to that horrendous experience, I had a *process*. You couldn't tell me anything. My buddies were like, man I want to try and look like that. I remember telling them about the product, but not telling them about the experience. They found out for themselves.

About that little girlfriend across the street, my *process* took away some of my shyness with her. But again I'm telling you, my being shy seemed to be a constant factor that kept reminding me and would continue to plague me as a part of my emerging personality. And there was Pamela who I went to elementary school with back in Cherry Hill. Now remember that we have moved uptown on the West Side but she would catch two Baltimore City Transit buses to come and be with me. We would fool around a little down in the basement where I slept at this time. I still wasn't as comfortable as I would have liked to have been in regards to my *shy issue*. A little bit later, I would reciprocate the visit and go back out to Cherry Hill to see her. She told me that she had a former boyfriend that had difficulty in letting go. So she asked me to come out there and be a male presence, to help with that situation. Now again, I was never a tough guy but only at certain times I would show up and act as if I was Billy Bad Ass, and I repeat, it was just an act. However, usually, I would typically illustrate the timid guy. Can't figure that one out.

Looking back, I definitely was a follower and not the leader type of a kid. As I was growing up, I acted as if I couldn't think for myself and

Summer Tours

needed others to sort of define me. Basically, I wanted to just fit in and belong. I wasn't close to anyone in my family growing up and today I understand it more. It wasn't personal as much as it was cultural. I know that I wasn't the only one that did practically what everyone else was doing. Not sure if it was peer pressure or just lack of courage to step out in my own identity. Throughout junior high school I wasn't as much of a ladies' man as I would become in high school (let me tell it).

During middle school, I did start my research in popping pills, drinking wine with the boys, and trying to stay out of trouble. I didn't see anything wrong with my behavior and felt that this is what kids do. After getting suspended a few times, I allowed that fact to influence my decision in choosing the high school I would attend. I did not purposely want to displease my mother, it's just that most of the decisions I was making resulted in that. Therefore, motivated with the intent to please my mother, I decided to go to an all-boys school way over in East Baltimore called *City High School*. I believe that my mother had reached her limit having to get me back in school from suspensions a multitude of times. The reasoning behind this decision was that if I could get away from the boys I hung around with in school, then maybe I wouldn't be influenced in ways that would keep me in trouble, one kind or another. I did not realize that wherever *you* go, you take *you* with you!

I began my embarking on a new direction by placing myself is this very strict school, clean on the other side of town. One bright note that resulted from this decision was that they had an all-girl school directly across the street name *Eastern High School*. The school turned out to be too strict for me. I didn't bother to do any research so I didn't have a clue what I was getting myself into, just to please mamma. I wasn't feeling that school at all except when I made the varsity swimming team and swam a few competitions, the few times that I was actually in school. I was very proud of that achievement to make the varsity team in the 10th grade. I and one other kid in the 10th grade made varsity that year and his name was Ricky Tate. I would later get the news about my friend being tied to a chair to be executed by getting his head blown off. That really saddened me and made me further realize the danger that lies await in the streets of Baltimore, even at a young age.

CHAPTER 3

Harlem Avenue

Let me backtrack a little. After leaving the projects and migrating to the west side of Baltimore, life began to take on a new meaning as I begin to approach my teenage years during the mid-60s. When my family left Cherry Hill, I was passing to the 6th grade. As previously mentioned, it was a common occurrence for Black families that spent a certain number of years in the projects, to move from South Baltimore to either West or East Baltimore (uptown). I was excited, not knowing what to expect, but looking forward to the next adventures for my young life.

The 1964 Presidential Election was upon us and I recall while we were playing in the schoolyard, we were discussing what we thought about going back to Africa. Barry Goldwater, the Republican nominee, was pledging to send us back there if he won. We were pledging as kids, even at that age and the climate of the times, we took a very opinionated position, at least I know that I did, "No we're not going." I don't know how that would have played out but he lost to Lyndon Johnson that year. Taking a position on political topics of the day while in the 6th grade gave me a heads-up on how outspoken I would develop

YOUR DECISIONS DETERMINE YOUR DESTINY

into being. As a matter of fact, Mamma reminded me on more than one occasion, "You always got a lot to say." I believe I frustrated her even early on, with my eager ability to express myself.

Honestly, we were all relieved that we didn't get shipped out particularly since we didn't have a clue what Africa was about except the Tarzan movies we watched on television. We surely weren't taught anything positive or glorious about Africa in school, by design. I began to notice I had some organizational skills even in the 6th grade during our basketball tournament. Along with the other four guys on our team, I began to strategize a pathway to victory. Perhaps the old saying is true: "Leaders don't wait for permission." I'm not completely sure how I came up with my ideas, but they worked. We took the championship title that year. I had a few great kids on my team and with a little coordination they made it happen. I was just very proud to be a part of that experience.

When we first arrived at our first house, 2723 Harlem Avenue, it didn't take me long to start meeting a lot of people in my neighborhood and start experimenting with different things for acceptance. Of course, I had to be sneaky with things I had no business fooling around with. A few guys on the block seemed to be a little *faster* at the street life than I was. Unlike the Project Community, the houses on each block were in a row side by side until that particular block ended by a side street, and then picked back up on the other side of the side street. Ex: 2600, 2700, and 2800 block respectively. These new friends were a bit different from my previous childhood buddies. They had already preceded me on this entirely new level of the *inner city* life. These guys were even going away to reform school, fighting regularly and to me, they looked like they weren't afraid of anything. A few of them had names like Joe Bean, *Hardrock, Wheppie, Yerbie,* and *Baby Lip*. Then I noticed another group a little bit older around my brother Poochie's age that reminded me of some scenes I eye witnessed back in Cherry Hill. I watched some dudes fistfight and beat the police up with their bare hands without a speck of fear in their heart. Uptown on Harlem Avenue, I witnessed a few bad dudes from another area come to fight these older guys on my block. It wasn't so much of a *gang war* as it is in other cities, but more of a different side of town beef. Guys like Levi, Blind Henry, Eddie, and Pete.

Harlem Avenue

These guys worked out regularly and showcased the physiques to prove it. We used to pass through the alleys and would see them pumping that iron in blind Henry's backyard, one block up the street from us.

Anyway, one of the *out of the neighborhood* guys had a gun and I witnessed him shooting at Levi as Levi was rushing towards him, right in the middle of the block. Levi somehow absorbed the multiple rounds entering his body, continued rushing the guy, took the gun, and began beating him down and kicking the guy under a parked car. I thought to myself, that is one baaaaad dude there. They obviously gave the visiting dudes a whipping I'm sure they never forgot.

As I was entering into junior high school I started smoking cigarettes more, drinking a little wine here and there, cutting class as such was the norm at that time in my life. I really didn't take junior high school that serious and did the bare minimum just to keep momma off my back. I remember one time I took a teargas/blank gun to school, that I *borrowed* from my brother Carroll, (without his knowledge). I just wanted to show off and try to represent an image that really wasn't me. It really didn't seem like that much of a big deal. My seventh-grade teacher Mr. Winder heard me fooling around with it and demanded that I produce it. It was making some type of clicking sound that he obviously knew for sure; there was a real need for concern. Of course, I got immediately nervous as all eyes focused on me upon his request. I was a bit hesitant but felt compelled to comply with this demand. As a result I was taken straight to the office and suspended until my parents came to the school to make things right.

My grades at the time were satisfactory, that is when I was paying attention, and remaining focused. I used to enjoy clowning around a lot in school, despite the threats from my dear mother. I seemed to always think that I was a bit smarter than everyone else was so therefore my complete undivided attention was not necessary, (so I thought). During one of the times that I was sent to the office for *cutting up*, when no one was looking, I decided to open some of the drawers that where in the office just to see what was there. Just being nosey. To my delightful surprise, I discovered a pack of blank report cards for each of the quarters. I stole a pack (one

YOUR DECISIONS DETERMINE YOUR DESTINY

report card for each quarter) and began to bring report cards home that I myself graded. Now I knew even back then that it would not be wise to be excessively generous with my grades as to not arouse suspicion. Like most parents, a lot of good rewards came along with good grades. I was the man, you couldn't tell me nothing. For a while, I was floating high on a cloud of deception and obviously, it didn't bother my conscience not one bit. Mamma was so proud and seemed to have backed off me a bit.

Meanwhile, my dear one and only sister Vonnie, God bless her heart, was a bit jealous and envious of the rewards I was reaping from my fraudulent good grades, as I probably would have been too if the situation was reversed. One of my dear momma's many favorite sayings was, (what's done in the dark, will come to light). Obviously, I wasn't as slick as I thought I was. For some scary reason I decided to hide my original report cards under the carpet in the dining room just in case, for whatever. During the process of vacuuming and perhaps even shampooing the dining room carpet one fine day, my sister discovered my secret. For her, it was like winning the lottery because instead of being humble while I was being deceptive, I was gloating with a bit of arrogance. Vonnie ran to my mother liked Jesse Owens running down the track. I had to be around 13-14 at the time, my dear sweet mom, who was the disciplinarian of the house, tried to crucify me. I believe she was more upset with the fact that I deceived her than some of my grades not being up to par. I felt ashamed and embarrassed only because I got caught, but had not my sister exposed my trickery, I'm sure I would have never confessed, at least not anytime soon.

At this time, I didn't really get into a lot of trouble in the streets but I was more and more aligning myself with, and being defined by, the people I hung around with. I was a thin, timid type of guy. I wasn't the one looking to prove how *bad* I was, because I wasn't. I was always a very shy guy when it came to the girls, and that fact always frustrated me. I had many opportunities after my first time to get close to a lot of girls but failed to do so as a result of my shyness, which lasted well into my adult life. I began to feel that something unique was wrong with me and had no clue how deep my shyness ran. No matter how hard you try, it becomes very difficult to change your reality into something different, overnight.

Harlem Avenue

Movie theaters were all over the place and I found myself quite often going to the movies by myself. It wasn't that I couldn't get a date; I think it really didn't bother me that much at that time and so I just rolled with the flow. I started becoming a loner and didn't feel any *particular way* in being so. On several occasions, I used to go downtown and catch a Greyhound bus to New York City. I would reach Port Authority, the bus terminal, and then begin to travel from 8th Street and 42nd Avenue. I was particularly attracted to a lot of the rated R theaters, which were lined up almost right next to each other all the way up the street, and across the street on both sides. One block over on 43rd Street was the same movie lineup. It was fascinating to me to see all of those movies congested in a set area. I would imagine that there were at least 30-40 or more movie houses in this one section. I would set in one for a while and then go check out another one. I developed a fascination for adult movies at this teenager time in my life probably because I wasn't legally allowed to go see them, except in New York City where they didn't enforce age limits. In fact, this area was known as the *Forty Deuce*, or simply the *Deuce*. At the time, it was called "Cinema's most notorious block in the world."

After walking through Manhattan, I would walk west up 42nd Street until I reached the high rises (projects) at 42nd Avenue and 10th Streets. I was amazed at how tall the buildings were all over Manhattan. Being as I was from Baltimore, I tried not to be too obvious staring at the skyscrapers as if I didn't belong there. I didn't want to stand out although I'm sure I probably did anyway. I would then swing over to 43rd and 10th streets, sit on a bench, and just observe the day-to-day activities before my eyes. For some reason I felt comfortable in the *Big Apple*. I would spend almost the whole entire day in New York at 14, 15, and 16 years old and not one soul from Baltimore ever knew I was there.

It was a good thing that drugs hadn't become a major force in my life yet since I was hanging out in one of the major drug capitals of the world. I probably wouldn't have been able to leave there *unscathed* the many times I was able to. One of the worst things about making a decision to do something wrong and getting away with it, you continue to do the same. The bus ride from Baltimore to New York took approximately 3

YOUR DECISIONS DETERMINE YOUR DESTINY

1/2 hours and I used to take that ride as if I was just going downtown. I was very glad when I began coming out of that *phase* in my life. I started to become less shy and more into appreciating and enjoying the many girls that were *on* me. I seemed to have come into a kind of a *switch*. I went from a shy guy and now I wanted to be a *lover boy*. I probably was calling myself that, making up for missed opportunities.

A lot was going on in the country at this time and it was so much for a young person to choose from. There was the *hippie* movement, which I found myself dabbling with that experience for a while. Me and a couple buddies on my block used to go downtown to these hippie nightclubs where they had the black lights, psychedelic posters, and we already had either marijuana or maybe a little bit of acid to *rollout* with. Although Soul Music was the order of the day, I wanted to explore other genres and lifestyles at the time. Another phase I was to experience I guess just because it was there. I invested into a lot of hard rock albums to include groups like *Led Zeppelin, Deep Purple, Iron Butterfly, 10 Years After, Jimi Hendrix, Grand Funk, Chicago,* and the like. My family would hear this *noise* coming from the basement and wonder *what the hell is he listening to*? Accessorized with weed, some hard psychedelics drugs (such as acid, LSD, mescaline), and customizing the basement to look like a hippie den, a couple buddies and I would go on *trips* without leaving the basement.

Truthfully speaking, my investment into the multitude of albums I amassed was hardly any money from me. Back then, Columbia Records and Capitol Records advertised that they would send you 12 albums for one dollar if you join their club. So not only did I make the decision to join the club for one dollar, but also for about five or six alias names that all had my address, they also joined their club as well. So the decision to start cheating and the deceptive behavior had already been established. This resulted needless to say, in perhaps 75 to 100 albums that were acquired for just a few dollars. The albums just kept coming and of course, I wasn't the only one in on this scheme. You know the old lame excuse, (everybody else is doing it). Later on, they would attempt to track me down when I entered the Army, but then it was too late for them. The mind-set

Harlem Avenue

was how can I get something for nothing? How can I get over on the system? My justification was that *I didn't want to miss out on a good thing*. What decision can I make that would allow me to gain the rewards from hard work, without putting in the labor or paying the required cost?

CHAPTER 4

So Many Choices

Traveling through the various places and the special times that I had the opportunity to experience, presented a multitude of choices for a young teenager. Particularly growing up in the inner city of Baltimore, Maryland. Making a decision to hang out with my buddies, drinking a little wine, popping a few pills and what also came along was smoking a little marijuana during those days; it seemed to be the norm. The need to be accepted and a *part of* was increasingly apparent as I plunged into my teenage years. Obviously, my buddies and I at such a young age didn't have a clue what was waiting for us down the road as a result of experimenting with the *get high* scene.

At the early teenage season in your life, you almost begin to think that you're invincible. As long as you don't get caught, you think that you are big and bad enough to try almost anything. Whatever it may be, if one of my boys can do it, I can do it and perhaps more than they can. In the inner city environment that I was exposed to, it appeared to have its own standard of behavior already

YOUR DECISIONS DETERMINE YOUR DESTINY

established. Yes, my parents, like everyone else's tried to instill morals and standards into my knucklehead, but it seemed like what was going on outside of the house, particularly on the corner, was more attractive. Once you come outside, and meet on the corner, I think we were just captivated by the awaiting decision on what to do next. It's almost as if my decision was made by default, just an automatic pattern of *doing my thing*.

The corner can be described as a board meeting room where you meet regularly to lay out the plans for the company. It appeared to be a strong lure and it was difficult resisting that attraction. I could easily blame the lack of structure not provided by my father, however, the decisions always rested on me. Looking back, not one time did I ever entertain the thought of carving my own path and not following the crowd. For some strange reason, it just wasn't the thing to do. Once again, was it just influence under plain peer pressure or just an atmosphere established in the inner city living? My decision making process at this time in my life was never carefully thought out. Quite honestly, I never entertained the thought of carefully making *any* decisions from good information. Instead, I was impulsive and just flowed with the wind. Once again, I was a young kid with a mind that settled for being shaped by the atmosphere of the time. I can admit putting too much concern on what others thought about me as opposed to what I thought about myself. Perhaps because although I was competitive in various ways, it served to cover up that shy, skinny, timid kid that I really was.

As I noted earlier, the *Flower Power* movement, also known as *Hippies*, was a strong presence in society at this time. Now it wasn't as prevalent in the urban inner city neighborhoods as it was on the outskirts of the city, however, its influence somehow made its way into the fabric of African-American neighborhoods. Record albums were the music media and the radio stations we listened to that only came through the AM band were W.W.I.N; W.S.I.D; and of course another very popular broadcasting radio station owned by none other than the *God Father of Soul*, superstar *James Brown*. His radio station name was W.E.B.B., which stood for *We Enjoy Being Black*.

So Many Choices

Eight track cassettes were just coming on the scene and were very popular for a while. However, the media player of the day was record players that played either 45 disc or complete albums (33s). Although I went through my Hippie phase for a summer, my brother Poochie always played some good strong *soul* music in the house, as well as a little jazz at times. I believe my decision to go with the *rock music* seemed to fit perfectly with the drugs I was increasingly using. It also seemed to go along with my scarf wrapped around the middle of my forehead and *Afro*, my psychedelic bleached out jeans, and my peace symbol medallion hanging around my neck. I thought I was a black hippie for a minute. Music was a very strong part of the fabric that was woven into our communities. Drugs ran real close behind the music and we cannot omit the fact that there were liquor stores all around. We had to go downtown where they sold rolling papers for your weed that came in various delicious flavors. Banana, lime, cherry, chocolate, and so on. They also had these fancy pipes that you could buy from the *head shops* from downtown to smoke your weed and *hash* in. Some of those pipes were very exotic with multiple long hoses extended from the base so that multiple people can smoke at the same time from the same pipe. The design probably came from the Far East especially since our involvement in the Vietnam War was heavy at this time. I felt good growing up at in those days not even realizing that a time such as that will never be repeated again.

Another choice that had an even stronger presence in the neighborhoods was called at that time *The Black Muslims*. The late great Malcolm X was killed in the year of 1965. His strong influence was not only on the Nation of Islam, but profoundly on the Black Community as well. His ideology and black consciousness theme was a much-needed uplift for the people of color at this critical time in history. The nation of Islam philosophy was and still is self-sufficiency through cultural and economic empowerment. Then, those brothers were posted up more than what you may see today, with their dark sunglasses, bow ties, and all suited up, it was a sight to behold. Out on the streets everyday selling their newspapers originally named *Muhammad Speaks* and then later named *The Final Call*. They also sold these bean pies as a way of generating

YOUR DECISIONS DETERMINE YOUR DESTINY

much-needed funds. They are so well respected that even in the penitentiary's across the land, they maintain a strong and cohesive presence. There is no doubt that the white powers that be, had to yield a considerable amount of respect and admiration for a strongly established entity, within the circumference of this country. Of course they would and still do attempt to slander the organization at any opportunity that presented itself.

At the very same time, the Black Panther party was at its height in this country, from coast-to-coast. This organization as with the Black Muslims advocated a much-needed self-reliant and independence from the *man* that began to guide the thinking of an oppressed people effectively. The Black Panther Party's militancy was only a reaction to the outright brutality of the police and law enforcement that was inflicted on people of color. It was never a problem when everyone else utilized the 2nd Amendment. However, when it came to African-Americans constitutionally establishing the right to bear arms; the U.S. Government had a big problem with that prideful, confident look that the Panthers displayed. These brothers and sisters with their all black outfits, to include leather jackets, and black *tams*, represented a black power pride that to this day have never been publicly displayed in such a manner. The climate of racial injustice provoked such a response from a proud people, despite the accusations and outright lies. They marched in a disciplined military formation with their weapons displayed with a fierce commitment.

The real true story came out later how through President Nixon's administration and Edgar J. Hoover's FBI bureau, (and it did belong to Hoover), deliberately and systematically staged shoot-outs with the Black Panthers to the extent of their elimination. The government's superior weaponry had the clear dominant advantage. The insurmountable fear that motivated the government of these Black Warriors revealed that White America could not and would not tolerate such a bold distinction of Black pride that was willing to protect their own, at any cost. It appears that the US Government conceded to the fact that just the mere picture of these warriors and what they represented was definitely

So Many Choices

not, what the *founding fakers* had in mind. It was not advertised that one of the cofounders of the party, Huey P Newton, earned his PHD degree in Social Sciences.

Their focus was also on the immediate needs of the community such as food and clothing. The Black Panthers regularly held food drives, which fed the schoolchildren and adults in the neighborhood. In fact, some of the high schools in Baltimore would allow representatives of the Black Panther Party to come to the auditorium and give a speech, Edmondson High school, that I attended, was one of them. I remember getting so pumped up after their speeches that I was ready to go out and start a revolution all by myself. One of the girls I was dating in high school actually joined the Panthers. Novelair Peele. I recall when we use to hook school and I took her to our house, (after getting better with the shyness), I had to wrestle with her just for a kiss. I have to say that it wasn't an easy match for me just because she was a girl. My girlfriend was a little tough. She was about serious business and committed to the cause of Black pride and liberation.

Of course, I can't leave out the non-violent movement of the late great Dr. Martin Luther King Jr. His well-known peaceful, passive resistant to civil injustice and oppression was a stark contrast to the militant and Muslim approach to the social climate of the day. Martin was so effective in promoting change that the FBI named him as *one of the most dangerous men in America*. Can you believe it? A Baptist preacher deserving of that title? His effectiveness, along with his comrades, mobilized the masses of people (of all races) in a way that has never, ever been seen before in this country. His commitment to uplifting the poor and oppressed people, particularly in the Deep South, was unprecedented. His message rang loud in the hearts and minds of multitudes of people that had any kind of conscious. When Martin spoke and gave his speeches, it seemed to touch you in a special way that could not be denied. His strong influence on the masses of people proved threatening to the powers that be. He was definitely one of my heroes as well as so many others. In my first book *Life, Love, Liberty,* I wrote a great poetic tribute in his honor rightly entitled:

YOUR DECISIONS DETERMINE YOUR DESTINY

Marvelous Martin

Now Martin had a dream he was led to share
To show the whole world, how much he cared
His aim wasn't to cause a lot of trouble and strife
But to righteously improve, our quality of life.
Look how he struggled to get his point across
And his original purpose, still was not lost
He was sought after, beaten, and thrown in jail
But so divinely driven, he could not fail.
Peace was in his heart, so he didn't hate any
Just wanted to represent the oppressed, which was so many
Even went to the White House, to witness the signing of a bill
All he ever strived for, was to do God's will.
Back in the Sixties, confusion was at no end
But throughout it all, emerged a true friend
Despite all the accusations, despite all the lies
Martin still came out with, a Nobel Peace Prize.
Dear Martin we thank you with our deepest affection
For the beauty of your dream, showing us the right direction
Dear God, you seem to know just when to send
Someone that the whole world could call a true friend
Through Your wisdom
He became quite clever
Like you will do for any of us
That will praise you forever.

So Many Choices

The dream he had was our dream and no one else could best articulate and express that shared dream. In response to his assassination on April 4th, 1968, Black people went into a sort of *unacceptable* mode that resulted in riots, looting, and major fires from coast to coast. I remember saying to myself, "Here is a very peaceful, non-violent much needed leader, and they are going to kill him. Screw the law." Right then and there I plainly understood why Black folk burn and loot in response to a major civil blow.

"Why destroy your own community?" the question would ring out. Most Black folks understand that first of all, it's not their community. It belongs to the merchants and the police. I have personally heard the cops after rolling up on the corner many times telling us "Get off my corner." Can you understand how powerless that would make you feel *supposedly* in your own neighborhood? Can you empathize with that experience? Oh, I get it. It's difficult to understand or respect an experience that you can't personally relate to or identify with. What some people would do instead is judge or impose a moral standard of their own that doesn't quite fit the situation. I was 15 at the time and yes, I decided to participate in the looting as the opportunity presented itself. I too went in a couple of Jewish clothing stores that were located in the *hood*. I had a whole bunch of these particular slacks that were in style called *Shadow Stripes*.

I remember feeling a sense of cultural pain upon hearing of his murder. My heart, like so many others across the nation was broken. That was the last straw. It was a cultural reaction that exploded from not only the assassination but from the culmination of hundreds of years of oppression and injustice. PHD Scholar Dr. Joy Degruy classified it as *Post Traumatic Slave Disorder*. I'm so glad that we have empathetic scholars that are educated enough to call it what it really is instead of the media and others calling it by what makes them comfortable. I remember my mother telling me not to participate in the riots, yeah, ok mamma. I made the decision to join in anyway. Of course, her concern was me not getting locked up. My brother Poochie was in the Army and my sister Vonnie wasn't about to go out and *loot*. I was all in with the rest of the country. What eventually stopped us was Martial Law was imposed that prohibited anyone being on the streets at first after 6 pm and then eventually past 12 noon. In Baltimore, they had the National Guard and

YOUR DECISIONS DETERMINE YOUR DESTINY

the Green Berets posted up to enforce the Martial Law. This was the first time I experienced tear gas in a riot setting. My eyes burned a little and were very irritated. I guess we were a little lucky in Baltimore. At least we didn't see Army Tanks rolling down the streets as they were doing in Newark, New Jersey at the time.

When I did attend my first choice of high school, it wasn't a decision based on the right motivation, and I just wasn't open minded enough to give it a good chance. After a few days in school, I put in a request for transfer in which they denied. That was another opportunity to show the utmost disrespect for the authority figures in my life. I remember thinking, "You won't transfer me, I won't attend." Mail would come to the house to my mother from the school each month stating how many days I missed for that month. It would usually be almost the entire month checked off. My mother would get me back into school after being suspended for that abundance of absences, and as soon as she would leave, I would catch the next bus and come back to the West Side of Baltimore. Sometimes I would go downtown to the Federal Building at Hopkins Plaza and join the Black Panthers for a protest rally. I would just fall right in sequence while they were marching around the government building. Or maybe go to my buddy Earl's house where his mother Mrs. Smith, God bless her soul, would allow myself, Joe, Enoch, and Earl to hook school the majority of the school year. I believe her reasoning was that she would rather us be in her house than to be out in the streets getting into trouble.

I realized at the time that a person can do wrong for so long, that the wrong actually begins to *look* right to them. I was there. As time went on, we were all worried about my brother Poochie who was drafted into the Army, along with so many of my friend's older brothers. Almost all of them were sent to Vietnam. Statistics would later reveal a very high presence of young African-American soldiers out in the bush assigned to the infantry division, in Vietnam. Those that made it back shared with my friends and me a lot of stories of the experiences they encountered.

My transfer for my requested high school finally came through a year later. Needless to say, that in my first tenth grade experience I was left back, simply because of the fact that I was absent almost the entire school

So Many Choices

year. Yet, I somehow made the varsity swim team and enjoyed a couple of swim meets the few times I was present in school. I obviously did what interested me and what didn't, I wasn't there. That second 10th grade experience at the new school was a piece of cake. I not only made the Honor Roll a couple times to show my mother I can do it, I also called myself a *lover boy*. The innate shyness was still very present, I guess my hormones at 16 began to override the shyness and were declaring that it's time to *get this show on road*. I had multiple girlfriends and was finally catching up where *I* thought I should have been long ago. I guess some of us are just slow starters in certain areas. Finished the 10th, finished the 11th, and I was bored. It just wasn't working for me anymore. I was beginning to feel like school was a waste of time and I needed somethin' different. Now here comes a very serious decision and one that would have a very profound effect on my life for many passing years. Naturally, I always had the option of choosing to do the right thing. I believe that I was so caught up in the flow of things, that making a good sound decision based on reliable information just wasn't the order of the day for me.

CHAPTER 5

The U.S. Army

After hanging in the streets for a period of time and enjoying a couple of different girlfriends, the high school scene had completely lost my interest. I only had but one more year of high school, I repeat just one more year, and then I would be finished. The Service Draft (forcing you to serve in the military) was still in effect in 1971 and my thinking was that I'll probably get drafted just like my brother before me, and my father before him. As noted earlier, a lot of the good stories I heard from my brother and my friend's brothers about their service experiences, left a very impressionable picture in my mind. For instance, my brother Poochie used to send back home pictures of little cute Cambodian girls sitting on his lap in a nightclub looking like they were having the time of his life. At age 16, I thought, man that's got to be the life. That was enough incentive for me. Now mind you, I wasn't thinking about any Combat Infantry stuff, but only the girls and the marijuana, which was a big appeal to me. Since the draft was still going on, when I turned 17 years of age, I decided to join and all that I had to do was to get my parents to sign the entry papers that I brought home.

YOUR DECISIONS DETERMINE YOUR DESTINY

Unaware to my knowledge, I would find out that they ended the draft one year later for good. I had just finished the 11th grade and that summer Mamma signed the forms so that I could enter the Army. To my surprise, she sort of snatched the papers out of my hand and signed them immediately, which prompted me to ask her, "Don't you want to think about this a little bit, mamma?"

She quickly said; "No, you need to go do something good with your life." Little did I know that decision would open several doors for me way down the road. Now my thinking was, instead of wasting nine months in 12th grade and not be paid, I could get my GED in three months time in the Army and be paid for it. Brilliant right? So I thought. Back then, you didn't need to finish school like you do now to go into the service. So I signed up for the Army and it had to be the Army so I could follow suit from my father and my brother's footsteps. Besides, the Marines were a little bit too crazy with their training for me and the Navy wasn't an option, too much water. The Air Force could have been a possibility, but I strongly felt that my decision was already laid out for me. My father served in France and Belgium during WWII fighting the Germans and my brother Poochie served in Southeast Asia, Saigon, Vietnam.

When it was time for me to leave home and catch the bus to go in, I almost had to fight my girlfriend Sharon off me so that I could board the bus. She was fighting desperately for me not to leave her. At 17, I was very much sweet on her, but not enough to keep me from going to the next step in my life. My mind was made up. My decision was final. Also, I need to add that she wasn't the only *heart* that I was leaving behind. We were holding the bus up long enough with our romance drama until I heard someone on the bus shouting out, "Girl, will you let that man go?" I was truly thankful for that impatient intervention; we were creating a bit of a scene. Although I was still a boy at the time, she finally surrendered to the fact that she couldn't persuade me to stay and released me from her frantic grip. But she surely gave it her all and all as I'm sure, the entire # 15 Baltimore Transit Bus passengers headed downtown could testify.

Once my mind is locked in on something, it's almost like a heat seeking missile destined to hit an unavoidable target. It is nearly impossible to

The U.S. Army

get me to change course. I didn't have a clue what I was getting myself into. Sometimes when you imagine or project something to be a certain way, it turns out to be quite different. This was very true how I perceived entering into the US Army.

First, I was assigned to Fort Dix, New Jersey for my Basic Training. I pretty much breezed through it because before I went in, I ran a lot of *whole court* basketball games. So I was in decent physical shape. I couldn't boast of any noticeable muscles with my thin frame except my natural abs. I did go in with an eight pack that I was very proud of. In fact, my abs could be distinguished from across the street even with a T-shirt on. The psychological indoctrination that you are first exposed to was a bit of a challenge for a slim, somewhat of a timid guy as I was when I first showed up. Right from the start, I thought these *jokers* were out of their mind getting up close and personal screaming in your face. I did feel a bit intimidated in the beginning. It was funny and scary at the same time for me. These guys were focused and I knew for sure that I had stepped into their world. Then I began to catch on to the tactic of breaking you down so that they can build you back up, *their way*. Obviously, some guys just couldn't *cut the mustard*, which resulted in them *bombing out* of boot camp. An intense physical and psychological assault came straight at you. I'm sure that all the other Armed Forces had their *rejects* as they were called, as well. I guess not everything is for everybody. A few even made their exit by way of the Stockade (Army Jail) and then they were released from the Army.

I fell in love with the M-16 rifle and qualified as an Expert on the range. I guess you never know how good you are at something until you're given the opportunity to try it out. It's a lightweight automatic rifle, which houses different capacity magazine clips. I had an idea that while I was in Boot Camp to steal a M16, bury it out in the woods wrapped in some plastic, and then go back and retrieve it once I was finished with my Basic Training. There was one *snag* in this plan. How am I going to be granted permission to enter back into Ft. Dix and walk back through the gate, even if the weapon was completely disassembled? I'm glad that I thought that decision carefully through or I would have also been one of those that exited by way of the Stockade. I just wanted to cast a little light on my defiant, rebellious, and criminal thinking at the time.

YOUR DECISIONS DETERMINE YOUR DESTINY

Baltimore had such a bad reputation with crime in the streets. When I stepped into the *grenade toss box* to learn how to throw a grenade properly, the Drill Sergeant asked me where I was from. I told him Baltimore, and then his reply was, "Oh, you already know how to throw these." The DI had jokes. We had a bunch of crazy drill instructors at Ft. Dix that were fresh out of the jungles of Vietnam. I could see the lasting impact that the war had on these guys. From what I could observe, I don't think some of them ever detached from the realities of the jungle warfare they experienced to connect with their current reality of training. They were dead serious about teaching you how to kill and even more almost fanatical in teaching you how to stay alive at the same time. Who else could best teach you something that they just recently experienced? I still thought that they were crazy.

I still had a desire to volunteer and go to Vietnam, even though for the wrong reasons. Remember I'm not thinking combat and infantry and all that crazy stuff, I'm thinking girls and getting high. I went into the Army with my own agenda. Part of our Basic Training was for them to show us real life combat scenes videos where some of the guys were getting their heads cut off. The Viet Cong were using some of the most clever and diabolical booby trap devices designed just lying on the ground. The poisonous *Punji Sticks* that you step on covered with leaves and branches cleverly positioned in holes in the ground and the small zip top from a soda can, you pick it up, you're dead. I soon experienced a *moment of sanity*. Girls or no girls and weed or no weed, those images stayed in my mind for a while and that was just a training film. It wasn't a joke over there. I made a clear decision to abort that silly notion of deploying over into Southeast Asia. So because I signed up and didn't get drafted, I was led to believe, (deceptively) that I can choose where I wanted to be assigned to. Okay, I picked Panama for my overseas assignment and California for my state side assignment. It didn't happen.

Going through eight weeks of basic training at Fort Dix came to an end. The next assignment was my *Advanced Individual Training* also known as (AIT) which led me to Fort Jackson, South Carolina. This was my first experience of flying and it took us around 45 minutes flying

The U.S. Army

out of Baltimore. As I walked through the airport headed towards my departure gate, I was a little nervous but I was *all the way in*. By the way, after knocking off a couple of those little miniature whiskey bottles on the plane, I was in the air way before the plane ascended. I recall before I entered into the service a veteran telling me, "If you want an easy job, I suggest you get into supply or clerical work." I chose clerical work since I had a little typing experience under my belt from high school. This course was also eight weeks long like the Basic Training time.

My buddies and I went off post frequently to get high drinking and smoking weed as often as possible. I'm starting to adjust and fit in to this completely new way of life. The military is as different from civilian life as night is from day. At least that was my perception. My buddies and I did the nightclub thing on post and off post. As I stated, the course was eight weeks long. However, if you were able to graduate before the eight week period, that would get you off unpleasant duties such as KP, cleanup duties, and guard duties. I and one other soldier, a white guy, were the only two that finished the course in five weeks instead of the established eight weeks. But we still had to hang around for the rest of the class to graduate. Some were assigned to Germany and Korea, but most went to Vietnam. Just missed it! This was in the fall of 1971 and the US had two more years of ground troop involvement, not to mention that the enemy was gaining much ground as the war progressed.

As a result of my comrade and me graduating early, they decided to bless us with the favor of sending us to Alaska. I remember a sergeant at the base telling me with a little (I feel sorry for you) grin on his face, "Six months darkness, and six-months light." I didn't have a clue of what the hell he was talking about, until I arrived in Northern Alaska. We both were sent home on leave for a while and then were to meet back up at an Air Force base in Washington State. I had received my orders when I went home on leave. At first, I thought that I was going to an Air Force Base in (Washington, D.C.) until a neighbor came to me on the day before I was to leave and informed me that the base was located in Washington State. So I flew on a TWA flight from Friendship Airport out of Baltimore which was a non-stop 6 hour flight to Washington State. I watched a good movie on the plane part of the way called *Paint Your Wagon*.

YOUR DECISIONS DETERMINE YOUR DESTINY

I met the other guy that was at Ft. Jackson at the Air Base when I arrived. We spent the night and from there the Air Force flew us to an Army Base called Fort Richardson, Alaska, which is located in the very southern part of this frontier. I believe about 5 to 10 miles outside of Anchorage, its major large city. It was cold but not as cold as I imagined. They had just one easy job for us there and since *my* MOS (Military Occupational Specialty) was 71B30 and the other guy's MOS was 71B20, I was automatically entitled to first choice for that position. What happened was, an elusive sergeant changed my orders, gave the other guy the position that I was entitled to have, and sent me about 900 miles north close to the Arctic Circle, I was furious but there was nothing I could do. This was my first known experience with direct racism. I felt powerless after landing in a strange land and thought to myself, "This just ain't right."

It was around 0° at Fort Richardson and following orders, I boarded another plane for my next stop, which took me to Fort Wainwright, which had a greeting temperature of 35° below zero. Before I got off the plane, which was a very large Pan Am 747 Jumbo Jet, I felt the temperature getting cold inside of the plane and I was wondering to myself, "What on earth is out there?" Keep in mind that I just left South Carolina. As we exited this particular plane, I took a deep breath out in the Artic air, why I don't know. The sensation that exhilarated my lungs was an experience that caught me off guard. I had one more stop to go headed north. They had to fly me in a chopper (helicopter) to Fort Greeley, which revealed a straight-up base temperature of 50° below zero, and this was in the month of November. They told me that the winter was just about to begin. I was dumbfounded. Never before had I even imagined cold weather to this degree, and being exposed to it.

All I could see from the chopper was mountains, moose, and a couple of Eskimo villages here and there. When I stepped off of that chopper, I thought I landed on the moon. As customary, I wore my dress green uniform for traveling to a new assignment. What was popular at the time was different color matching silk underwear sets. That was all I had on under my dress green uniform, landing in the Artic. Talk about being totally unprepared! What was I thinking and which Alaska did I think I

The U.S. Army

was flying into? Trying to be hip, slick and cool, but instead I was hip, slick, and a fool. I wasn't cool when I set foot on that Artic ground; I was c-o-l-d and with clutched arms around my upper torso, I was shivering as if I just stepped out of a freezer box. My thinking was, "What in the world have I got myself in?" Brilliant huh? Quit school and get my GED in the Army. Didn't see this in the plans.

CHAPTER 6
At the Top of the World

I arrived at my final destination, an isolated outpost in a strange land. My time of arrival was around 8:00 PM on a Friday night, and it was pitch dark, very cold and still. I really didn't know what to expect so I kind of played it by ear. It was a type of cold that you could actually *see*. The Artic frost in the air was unlike anything that I have ever experienced before. I didn't notice anyone hanging around outside and there was good reason. The brothers were already getting high in the barracks, and so I courteously introduced myself and joined them. When I walked into the room, a cloud of marijuana smoke permeated the room along with beer and wine adding to the festive spirits. They welcomed me into their circle after checking me out to make sure I was cool. I told them all that I was from Baltimore and from that point forward, I was tagged with the nickname Bmore, although I wasn't the only brother from Baltimore that was stationed at this base. For some reason, perhaps because I thought I was slick, hip and smooth, (let me tell it), the nickname seem to fit.

YOUR DECISIONS DETERMINE YOUR DESTINY

I shared a room with a brother from Cleveland that more or less *showed me the ropes*. His name was Russell Warren and he was actually drafted trying to wind down his 2-year commitment. It was about four different outfits stationed at this particular base consisting of 3-4 barracks. Brother Warren had already been there at least 6 months prior to my arrival. However, this particular room number 137, turned out to be the hangout room for the *hip and cool* brothers in the barracks, not because of me, that was just the designated spot. We partied halfway through the night since it was the weekend and I felt right at home. I said to myself, "This might not be too bad of a setup after all."

I woke up the next morning around 10 AM on a Saturday morning and it was pitch dark outside. I looked at my watch and I looked outside and asked my buddies, "What the hell is going on?"

Their reply was, "You missed the daylight." My sense of the norm was about to be completely rearranged. Baffled and confused, it's just 10 o'clock in the morning.

"How could that be?"

Once again, they repeated, "You missed the daylight; it came out around 7:30 AM and by 9:00-9:30 AM its pitch black again until the next morning." Now when they first gave me that information, it didn't quite register with my brain although I am aware of the fact that not only am I positioned at the very top of the world, there are many strange phenomena that occurs at this latitude.

Okay, the day is Saturday and its cold like you wouldn't believe. Now we do get very cold winters in Baltimore from time to time, I mean bitter cold around 0°, freezing in the Chesapeake Bay, and freezing some people's pipes in their homes. I'm talking about some brutal cold winters at times on the streets of Baltimore that you don't want to be caught outside in. That was the most I had experienced up to this point. Back at the compound, this is the weekend and so throughout the day we are basically drinking and smoking weed, trying to get to know each other. I fall asleep later that night. I wake up around 10 or 10:30 AM that Sunday morning. Pitch dark outside, once again. I'm like; "Come on now what the hell is going on up here?"

Their reply was the same as the day before, "You missed it again." So from Friday evening going into Sunday afternoon I have yet to see any daylight. I realized right then and there that I had landed into another world. The fact that I'm getting high the whole time since I landed I believed softened the blow as far as accepting this brand new bizarre reality. I'm *tripping* anyway.

I finally wake up early around 7 AM to report to my duty station that Monday morning and finally see this so-called daylight. It wasn't any sunshine at all, in fact, it was about an hour and a half of a heavy gray overcast and closing in on 10 AM, and it was done. Now I'm beginning to see what that sergeant told me in South Carolina, "Six months of darkness and six months of light." But what I've come to find out, it was more like 8 1/2 months darkness and maybe 3 1/2 months light in the region I was assigned to. The winters are extremely long. Just as it is down in the lower 48's, some winters are more extreme than others are. Didn't think I could handle it, I thought it was just too crazy. I would eventually come to experience not seeing the sun at all for two months straight at a time. Later facts would reveal that Alaska has the second highest suicide rate in the country. Particularly in isolated regions near the Arctic Circle where there is no sunshine for months resulting in prolonged darkness. The depression sets in at an alarming rate at high latitudes. Then there are regions in the short summer time where the sun shines for two months straight, non-stop. A complete reversal.

I had an easy job after they finally put me with the right unit. At first, they made a mistake and put me in NWTC (Northern Warfare Training Center), and I was glad that I wasn't with that outfit but for a short period of time. We had to go out in the mountains and do some serious Arctic Warfare training. The temperature had to be at least 40 degrees below zero. We would suit up in our Artic Warfare Gear (TA 50) which comprised of white fur hooded parka, white mountain fatigues (thickly insulated), white VB (Vaporizing Boots), and your Artic Mittens. Those VB boots kept your feet surprisingly warm. They had a little valve on

YOUR DECISIONS DETERMINE YOUR DESTINY

the outside ankle part of the boot. So we go out and do various exercises in preparation of having to fight a war in that type of environment. Exercises such as perimeter assessment, securing designated coordinates, and search and rescue detail. Now I am a young adventurous type of guy, however, these types of activities were not on my radar. It seemed like it took them forever to clear up the mistake. I remember thinking to myself; I might as well be in Vietnam.

My correct unit was HHC Headquarters and Headquarters Company. I worked directly with the Company Commander and the First Sergeant as the Company Clerk like the *Radar* character on the TV series *Mash*. "Now you're talking," I thought to myself. This is what I signed up for after getting a tip before I entered the service to go into that particular field. I did a report every morning that was called the *Morning Report* on DA Form 1, one of the most important documents in the US Army. It reflected the various changes of the unit the preceding day, signed by the Company Commander. It showed the unit's personnel numbers, assignment gains, assignment losses, temporary duty assignments, personnel on leave, personnel that are sick, personnel locked up in the stockade, and so on. A very, very important document with vital information. It had several copies and the front white copy eventually made it to the Pentagon. I was responsible for it every morning once I was put in my right unit.

The only way you could transfer out of Alaska at that time, you had to put in a transfer form called a 1049. Right before I arrived there (11/71), the only options were Germany, Korea, and Vietnam. Once I arrived for some reason, they dropped Germany and Korea. Vietnam was the only option to transfer out of Alaska and a lot of guys from the Deep South that was sent there, immediately put their transfer in. I seriously considered putting mine in because they were telling me that the winter is just beginning to start at 50 degrees below zero. I was thinking, "My God, what in the world can get colder than that? Are you kidding me?" At any rate, each and every transfer request for Vietnam was approved. I repeat every one. I'm the one that initiated the paperwork for the orders, so I knew beyond a shadow of doubt that if you wanted to transfer to Vietnam, doesn't matter what your MOS was, you are definitely going. We send you back home on leave first, and then strait to Nam. This stark reality pretty much illustrated the inevitable outcome of our involvement in the war, those last two years.

The stumbling block for the US wasn't so much military might, but political forces at play greatly influenced by the strong protest of the war back home. Back home the nation at large was fed up with the war and the pressure to withdraw eventually dictated the dynamics of the outcome, along with fighting an enemy that you can't see. The Viet Cong had a sophisticated tunnel network that extended from Hanoi in the North, almost all the way down to their long and hard fought objective, Saigon in the South. I was still holding resentments for what they did to me 900 miles south. Gave that easy job I was entitled to have down in the warmer Ft. Richardson, to the white guy and sent me up north. I didn't want to deal with this extreme cold anymore, I had it! I'm done! I typed my transfer up and had my mind made up that I would take my chances in Vietnam. I placed the transfer on *Top's* (First Sergeant) desk. I told him it's too cold up here for me, I'm out of here. Just got out of going to Nam when I graduated early from my Advanced Individual Training in South Carolina. Now I'm ready to volunteer and go because I'm angry and it's just too damn cold.

Providence would have it that the First Sergeant needed me to remain and do that job so bad that he offered me a Corporal promotion real quick and Buck Sergeant right behind it, real fast. At this time, we were keeping up with the war. We were losing badly and quite simply the Viet Cong was kicking our butt as they continued to advance down the Ho Chi Minh trail toward their long sought after prize, Saigon. Once they capture Saigon, (Checkmate) it's all over. I really didn't want to go even as I did the paperwork, but I reasoned within myself, why not? I processed the paper work for several of my buddies that I briefly got to know from the Deep South. They couldn't wait to get out of Alaska because of being exposed to warm weather the majority of their lives. Check this out. A couple of my buddies we sent over to Nam, finished their 13 month tour, were sent back to the states and shot me a letter up to Alaska saying, "Yeah man, Nam was a trip and I'm glad to be back stateside."

I had to do 18 months up there in the Artic and said, "Damn, I knew I should have went." Question is, would I have been one of those that made it out? I then began to reason with myself. I recall how worried my mother was when my brother Poochie was over there before I entered the service. I also remembered my Father telling me if I ever ran across any quick rank opportunities, without kissing anybody's ass, go for it. After some very serious deliberating on this issue, I decided to go back to First Sergeant Obeneger, an Irishmen and told him I'll take the deal and stay, consequently tearing up my transfer requests. He did in fact handed me the Corporal rank pretty fast, and right before I was to get the Buck Sergeant, I got myself into some trouble, and it seemed to be on a regular basis. They snatched the Corporal, Private First Class, Private E2, and busted me all the way down to Private E1, forfeited part of my pay, and extra duty on the outside chopping ice and shoveling snow. I thought about still going to Vietnam anyway since the quick rank deal didn't pan out. I'm ready to *welch* on my agreement even though losing out was totally my fault. I wasn't into owning up to the part that I played in my life yet. I was 18 years old and very defiant.

Maybe those Black Panther party magazines that I had a subscription for and pinned them on my wall had something to do with my attitude. Looking back, I can see how I was heavily influenced just by the imagery of the Black Panther Party. Those Black Beret's cocked on the side of their Afro's, the dark shades, the black leather outfits, and their defiant stand against the *man* with their weapons fearlessly displayed during a police arrest of a black person. To a teenager like myself, there was no other heroic display of courage anywhere. I would have never guessed in a million years that here I am one day I'm walking down the hallway of my high school with my friends, flirting with the girls and before I know it, I'm in Northern Alaska. I felt comfortable with my decision because once you are a G.I.; you just can't say I changed my mind without some serious consequences. Since I didn't take the time to do a little research on this strange new environment I find myself in, I really didn't know what to expect. The sudden shift from being a civilian to being a soldier wasn't that much of a problem. Particularly since I was getting high on a daily basis almost like back at home, however, the stakes are about to be raised a bit higher. I was completely fascinated and curious as to what might be waiting for me up ahead.

CHAPTER 7

Adventures Unimagined

———◆———

Settling down in a strange environment wasn't as difficult as I would have thought it to be. My first job was relatively easy. After work and sometimes during work, we smoked a lot of marijuana on a daily basis. More and more, as a result of making the decision to continually use on a daily basis increasingly, became my norm. There were times *before* work we got high in the room calling it *morning cocktails* and on occasion, the company commander by the name of Major Hunter, would stick his head in our room in the morning looking for someone, and would not say a word about the big cloud of smoke that filled the room. This particular CO was cool, unlike the next CO that would follow him. Unfortunately, he had made his major rank in the field of Vietnam and for him to keep that particular rank; he had to go back to *Nam*. Apparently, his rank wasn't recognized in an administrative setting. So I did his paperwork and he soon shipped out. The next CO wasn't as cool as I'll detail a little later.

YOUR DECISIONS DETERMINE YOUR DESTINY

During the long winter, the company that I'm assigned to now didn't *do the outside* that often, thank God. Moving quickly, going from one building to another was the way we had to roll. Unless there was a specific reason or concern for being outside, we otherwise stayed in the different buildings that were there. The chow hall was in another building as well as other necessary connections. I unknowingly developed a fast-paced walk and didn't notice it until I first came home on leave. I would be hanging out with my homeboys I left behind and when we headed to the liquor store to get our drink, I would be walking so fast ahead of them that they would have to tell me to *slow my roll*. I had forgotten that fast that I wasn't in the Artic at that time. I believe that it was the second time out of several, that I came home on leave that I met my sister Vonnie's firstborn, Tasha. She was a cute little thing but took a little time getting used to her *soldier uncle*. I'll explain a little later, why I was able to come home several times on leave from Alaska.

Back to the Artic, the weather was so cold that they would post current temperatures on the inside of the barracks doors to warn you how long to expose your skin to the elements. Getting down to around 70° below zero it was advised to not expose your skin no longer then 15 to 20 minutes. You would not just catch *frostbite*, but your skin would actually begin to deteriorate. At times, I would walk out the barracks door and walk right past these huge buffalos, who just were hanging around. The base wasn't fenced in so they would just wander on the compound just as they pleased; dropping these big *poop* disc's in the snow and then they would keep it moving. I managed to avoid that detail.

The room I shared with this brother from Cleveland was apparently the hangout room for the coolest brothers in the unit, as I noted earlier. Room number 137 is where it was at. During the long cold winter, we would play cards, drink wine and liquor, smoke weed, and talk a lot of smack. We had got our hands on a little small black and white TV set. It was able to pick up perhaps two or three local channels due to our location. This same roommate that I had, (Russell), worked in this little post office that we had on the compound. Remember, we were in the last two years of our ground troops in Vietnam. All letters coming from Vietnam, which by the way, didn't require any postage stamp,

Adventures Unimagined

he would hold up to the light to determine if any contraband was in the envelope. Those that were *holding*, instead of putting them in the intended mailbox, he would instead put them in his pocket and bring back to the room.

By this time, I was 18 years old. At this point I had never stuck a needle in my arm as I had seen a few of my buddies back in Baltimore do in the back of the alleys while others like myself, just drank wine and smoked a little weed. Now this is when I made the foolish decision to try it out. This was pure heroin straight out of South East Asia. I remember the brother shooting just a little bit in my arm, and I immediately overdosed. I vaguely remember them getting me up on my feet, shaking me hard, smacking me a bit trying to bring me around. I was knocking hard on death's door and yet I still made the decision to try it several more times. After all, I wasn't going to be the only one out of the few of us that *got down* with it, to punk out. Even if it killed me, just like it nearly did. That was surely a clear depiction of the insanity I was about to embark on.

A couple of those days that my roommate didn't work in the post office; the mail actually reached its intended recipients. I reluctantly assisted in carrying one of the guys out of the barracks on a stretcher that did overdose and die. It was a white guy and he had turned almost blue. I clearly remember saying to myself, "What a shame, to have to come all the way up here and OD." However, that still didn't deter me from doing what I was doing. I recall shooting up heroin different times and sweating profusely, I would then step outside for a couple of minutes and the sweat immediately froze on my face and around my neck. I used to take my fingers and nails and scrape the ice sheets off my face. Any moisture outdoors when it's cold enough immediately freezes. At around 35° below zero and colder, you would see what is called *ice fog*. Very small tiny ice crystals that sets in the air like regular fog, but an Arctic style fog. One of the prettiest but weirdest sites in the night sky is called the *Borealis Aurora* also known as the *Northern Lights*. These cold waves of light that are green, purple, reddish slowly moving across the night sky. It sometimes made you think that you were on another planet. It's caused by the magnetic energy emanating from the North Pole.

YOUR DECISIONS DETERMINE YOUR DESTINY

I was starting to get a little bored so I picked up a camera at the PX, and picked up a 32 automatic equipped with a shoulder holster. I must have thought that I was a gangster/photographer or something. Any rate, I started snapping a lot of pictures inside and outside, especially when the season changed. Outside the barracks, you have *plug-ins* just like you pull up to a parking meter. If you had a personal vehicle up there, you would have to take it to the motor pool and have a heater system connected to the engine and the battery. When you pull up your car, you would have to plug it in or else it would freeze. It was getting near the time for me to come home on another 30-day leave. I caught that 747 Pan Am flight out of Fairbanks and that ride from my compound to the Fairbanks Airport was very dangerous. Those icy narrow mountain ridges and cliffs will scare you to death. The outside wheels of one of my buddy's car would be no more than several feet to the edge at certain points. Snow everywhere and the drop would have to be 800 feet or more straight down. We would look at each other in the car on this dark winter night and without saying a word but clearly distressed in an unimaginable way. If we slip off at any point, *we're done*! This was a path not often taken by others, especially at night. I even had to pee during this one trip to the airport and I had to hold it the entire nearly 2 hour trip simply because, stopping wasn't an option.

I come back to Baltimore on leave in the middle of the winter. It was zero degrees back home and what is known as a bitter cold winter. I was just hanging out with a couple of my buddies back in the hood, standing outside. They were wrapped up with very heavy coats and hoodies on and I'm standing out there with a thin open jacket on. And although people riding by looked at me like I'd lost my mind, they just didn't know (at that time), that the weather felt like spring weather to me. I had gotten a bit of what they call *acclimated*, to the Arctic. Now I have seen the same eyebrow raised on my compound. During the summer and winter we had a little movie house and the nearby Eskimos was allowed to use it and our snack bar for entertainment. I remember seeing for the first time the *Poseidon Adventure*, and standing outside waiting for the movie to start. The Eskimos will be in line with light jackets on, some open and it was about 70° below zero. I was wrapped up with my Fur Hood Parker, facemasks, VB Boots (Vaporizing Boots) and thick mountain fatigues. You could barely see my face. I wanted to swing over and visit Russia, since it was only around 55 miles across the *Bering Strait*. A narrow waterway that separates Alaska from Russia. I don't believe our relations with the Soviet Union were too favorable at the time. Plus the fact I was strongly advised not to go, and so I made the smart decision and did not go. I may have caught a fishing trolley and made it over there but it was a good chance that I wouldn't have made it back right away.

One day I decided to go out and take some pictures with the limited light that was available. We had a ski-training site 25 miles northwest of Fort Greeley by the name of *Black Rapids*. So I took a 2 and a half ton personnel carrier truck from the motor pool and took off with my camera and tri-pod to capture some winter scenes. I made it to the ski-training site, took some good shots, one with me on a pair skis, but I was *fronting*, I could barely stand up straight. Talked with a few of the guys up there, asking them how were they making out up here and they showed me by sharing some of their psychedelic drugs with me. After taking some of their *acid*, I then wondered out into the nearby mountains, the air was so pristine, and the landscape so breathtaking, I think the drugs that I took had me absolutely convinced that I was in another world. Got some more good shots, jumped back into the truck, and headed back to the compound.

This was a trail, once again that wasn't often traveled. About half way on my way back, the battery went dead. I was just fine as long as I kept moving, when I was forced to stop, immediate peril! Unimaginable temperature for that day, without exaggeration, it was about 85° below zero. Black Rapids was north of my base and the weather there can turn vicious on you real fast. I'll be honest with you; I thought this was the end. I'm stranded out in the Artic wilderness, very deep snow off the side of the trail and no one around for miles and miles. Survival mode kicked in after I was thinking that I do not want to go out like this. The truck got super cold immediately. I have to get some heat. So I decided make me a little fire in the back of the personnel carrier. Apart from the trail I was on, the snow was at least 4 1/2 feet deep, but I had to get some dry branches that would burn.

YOUR DECISIONS DETERMINE YOUR DESTINY

As I'm struggling to get the branches in this deep snow, about 75 to 100 yards away from me I see a brown bear. I had weapons back at the compound, but none with me. I wasn't thinking or I just plain forgot that I'm in the wilderness. (Could it be the drugs?) Anyway, I gathered up as many branches as I thought I needed, went back to the truck, and proceeded starting a fire. At first, it was starting to work, but I noticed, every time I checked on that bear location, he seemed to be a little closer each time. He was very crafty in his approach probably surmising the situation. Now I know this got to be the end. I reasoned within myself that I quit high school last summer so I could come here and either freeze to death, or get mauled by this bear. An unimaginable predicament! The smoke from the dry branches was killing my eyes; I couldn't take it any longer. I had to come out of the back of this truck so that I could breathe. I didn't know exactly what type of branches I was burning in the back of a Personnel Carrier, I just knew that is wasn't working. Just as the bear was getting closer and closer, it just so happened that a guy in a jeep was coming down the trail. I didn't ask him where is he going, can I get in; I just dived in the jeep and told him keep it moving. That was just too close for comfort.

One of the required trainings everyone had to do up here no matter what unit you were assigned to on this compound was called *Winter Indoctrination*. What you had to do was get a little tent and sleeping bag and go camp out on a mountainside for a minimum of three or four nights of at least around 40° below zero to indoctrinate yourself with the climate. They asked me, "Private Middleton, did you do your Winter Indoctrination?"

"Yes sir," I replied, "here is my certificate." I typed it up myself and thought, they must be out of their mind to think I'm going to sleep on a damn mountainside. I got away with that one.

When they first erroneously put me in the wrong unit, NWTC Northern Warfare Training Center, one of their details was S & R Mission, Search and Rescue. Sometimes, some knuckleheads would get a big idea to go exploring, (perhaps like taking pictures) and get lost. I had to accompany one S & R detail and several miles out from our compound was this deep

Adventures Unimagined

gorge in the earth. Many years ago certain parts of Alaska experienced earthquakes. Some evidence remains. I can recall the detail I was with using a rope and arm and leg traversing upside down across this big split in the ground as if we were crossing a little stream of water like back in Basic Training. This is something altogether different. I remember once again, saying to myself, "They must really be out of their damn mind to think I'm going across on that rope." I did it anyway only because I felt safe with the unit and I had to stick with them. My only options were to remain there and wait, or go the long way around and perhaps get lost myself. Now that I think about it, I was very rebellious. We found them, there was actually two guys and we came back another way. I was so glad that they finally put me in the unit I was supposed to be in the first place. Thank God. Those jokers were nuts. I didn't sign up for that, although when you are a GI, you're government property. They don't have a problem making that clear to you.

CHAPTER 8

Let's Make Some Trouble

———◆———

I'm nearly 8000 miles away from home, I have to do 18 months at this outpost, and I began to get a little bored. My buddies and I are getting high every day drinking and smoking weed, once in a while popping a few psychedelics. Once again, this activity seems to be the norm. When I first stuck that needle in my arm, I couldn't have possibly imagined the magnitude of what lay ahead. Didn't have a clue that a bona fide drug addict was born. Although we didn't do the heroin as much as other substances, nevertheless, I was well on my way. The seed was planted and it was just a matter of time before the full development of my addiction would blossom right before my eyes.

One positive hobby that I chose to continue to cultivate was my photography. We had a photo lab that was accessible and so I had a buddy of mine teach me how to develop and print black-and-white photography. I proceeded to gather a nice collection of photos that I had

YOUR DECISIONS DETERMINE YOUR DESTINY

taken, developed, and printed. Because I developed most of the photos, I foolishly took pictures of a lot of drugs piled up in one position, when I was dealing. I took pictures of a pile of (drug money), and a couple of pics of these Eskimo girls we would sneak in the barracks, when the opportunity arose.

As noted earlier I purchased an automatic weapon for my personal *piece* and another buddy and I from Oakland, California, contrived some con games to get extra money. What we would do, we would go to one of two guys that was in a fight, taking a piece of paper that we had already wrote that the other guy had put out a little contract on him for a certain amount of money. Clearly wrote out and signed by the other guy, (with the help of our intimidation). Then we would offer the other guy that was in the fight, the same opportunity to place the contract on the first guy for a certain amount of money. I need to say that we were very convincing and promising them both if either squealed, they would be taken out in the wilderness and done in. Then we would go to the other guy informing him that the other guy offered us more money than him therefore he would have to raise his original (fee), or else he would be the one to get *hit*. Now I need to say, this was not my idea, but my man Jerry Irvine of Oakland, easily sold it to me. With my cooperation, he showed me how to become an instant con man. When my partner in crime would go back home on leave, he would return to the base with newspaper clippings on him wanted for robbing places in Oakland, before he escaped back to the base. The Company Commander began to get wind of our little con games and eventually we had to fall back.

There were a few Eskimo villages located not too far from our compound. As noted earlier, they will come on the post and take advantage of some of the features on our facility. The Eskimo people are comprised of different tribes. Some still hold on to their native customs and rituals, which I will get into later, and some are very Americanized resulting in many alcoholics. The more skilled Eskimo can build an igloo in a short amount of time. Inside of the igloo, they actually sleep and burn a single candle that keeps the inside warm enough and comfortable for them. The way they build a small entrance to the igloo is kind of a zig zag, designed to keep the cold wind out. Truly fascinating. To me, they remind me

Let's Make Some Trouble

of a cold environment type of Indian. From time to time, when we got lucky, we would put a fur hood Parker on the females and sneak them into the barracks. I can tell you that it wasn't happening all of the time. But when it did, we had some pretty good parties. Remember, one of the main reasons I joined the Army was to get my hands on a couple of those Cambodian girls my brother had, I wind up with a couple of Eskimo's instead. How do you figure that out?

I came up with the idea that since we smoked so much marijuana, why not sell it. Our main supply was coming through Canada and for a while, it was quite consistent. Seldom would we experience a dry period where a bunch of psychedelics would temporarily take its place. Stuff like LSD, acid, mescaline, quaaludes, speed, and the like. Marijuana was our preferred drug of choice. I used to think of myself as a problem solver so I reached out to a magazine company in California for some information. I sent for a pamphlet called *The Complete Guide to Growing Marijuana*. Don't forget that I'm slightly below the Arctic Circle in a very cold, very long winter. The pamphlet instructed me to build a *Germinating Box*. What that looked like was an aquarium with a piece of 2" x 4" going across the top of one side to the other, lengthwise. In the middle underneath this wood would be a light bulb attached to it, and of course some soil and the seeds down in the bottom. The soil in Alaska, under the snow and ice, is super fertile. It worked for a while and I had drawn a little blue print of its design and made the decision to hide it in my closet.

During one of the <u>several</u> shakedowns from the CID (Criminal Investigation Division) of my little metal clothing closet, a little film canister filled with marijuana fell out of my closet and rolled across the floor. It was real funny watching that little can, but a nervous situation as well. I, my roommate, and 2 or 3 CID agents all standing in the room searching through my stuff and all of a sudden, this canister hit the floor and everybody's eyes fixed right on it as it rolled from one side of the room to the other side. I thought to myself, "Here we go."

When the agents found my diagram of the germinating box, I remember the big smile that came across his face and saying, "Aha, let's see if we can find this box." They didn't. I had it in another room on

YOUR DECISIONS DETERMINE YOUR DESTINY

another floor where I knew suspicion wouldn't be an issue. I still received another *Field Grade Article 15,* which fined my pay, extra duty outside, restriction, lost some rank, the usual.

That still wasn't enough for me. For a good while, I worked directly for the Company Commander and the First Sergeant in the position of the Company Clerk. I made a report of all changes taking place in the unit the day before, as noted earlier. It also gave me access to thirty-day leaves taken in or not. (Light bulb moment!) I need to say when you're 18 years old, you're likely to take certain risks that have clearly dire circumstances, or perhaps it was just me. I would go to certain people I trusted and offer a deal that when they go on a thirty-day leave and return, they would still have those 30 days not charged if they pay me a certain amount of money. Now along with all the other crazy adventures I undertook this one was far more dangerous. Because I not only tampered with at that time, the most important form in the Army, DA Form 1, I also had to forge the Company Commander's signature on the dummy report I put together. I was 18 going on 19, that the only excuse I can make.

I sent myself home more than what I should have, so much that people back home didn't believe I was still in the Army. How could you still be in the Army when you are home as much as you are? My response was that I know people, (me). Once again, the CO and First Sergeant began to get a sense that something foul was happening right under their nose, but they just couldn't figure it out or prove anything. So they threatened to send me to Fort Leavenworth and they were dead serious. I believe what got me out of that, along with God's grace, was my ability and apparent effectiveness to *con* my superiors. I knew at that time one thing that the military dreaded more than anything else was any kind of Congressional Investigation. I evidently convinced them with clear conviction, that my family had contacted our congressman back home, the Honorable Parren J. Mitchell and gave him a full report on how they were attempting to unjustly court-martial and send me to Fort Leavenworth. I dropped names, dates, committees and they eventually pulled back from their intent. This campaign to court-martial me was led by the current Company Commander Major Haley, a hard nose CO. The truth of the matter was I continued to make trouble one way or

Let's Make Some Trouble

another and now to be doing it right in the Headquarters office under his nose was truly insane on my part. Throughout all my incredible adventures, I was successful in obtaining my GED, and took a couple of Black History courses. Can you believe it? Through much frustration, my superiors kicked me out of that Company Clerk position, and sent me to the Motor Pool.

The Motor Pool wasn't a bad assignment. This is where all of the compound vehicles are located and serviced. I was actually the Post Commander's driver for a while. This is where I learned how to drive a Jeep, which had four or five gears, can't exactly remember for sure. Two incidents stand out the most during that change. I remember signing out a small camper type of vehicle and driving up the mountains just to get out. The back of the vehicle had a type of hood on it with small windows on both sides of it and a window in the rear. I think it was the only vehicle available. So I'm driving up this mountain, smoking weed and I can recall seeing the clouds setting real low or either I was up on very high ground. I believe at that latitude, the clouds in the sky seem to set lower than they do down in the states. We are near the top of the world. Never seen anything like that before in my life. Coming down the mountain was very scary. Some of the ridges I drove down were like that trip I rode to the airport to go home on leave where my outside wheels were like 4 or 5 feet in some areas from the cliff, no guard rails. Once again, perhaps 800 to 900 feet drops. I never was so scared for my life. I hit a bump and that whole hood part in the back came loose and fell off the truck. I stopped and since I couldn't put it back up there, I pushed it over the cliff. When I got back to the motor pool, they was like, where is the rest of the truck? All I can say is that it fell off and that was that.

The other interesting experience I had while being the Post Commander's driver was when I received an order to go out to the air strip where the choppers land, and pick up these three VIP's. Instead of a Jeep, they told me to take the sedan car, still an Army vehicle with three speeds on the collar. The air strip was about 5 or 6 miles from the compound. Not too sure how I made it there not knowing how to drive a three speed up in the collar, but I did. It was a Brigadier General (1 Star), a Colonel, who set in the back, and a Lieutenant Col. who set up

YOUR DECISIONS DETERMINE YOUR DESTINY

front with me. As I proceeded back toward the compound, the Lt. Col. that was sitting up front with me was asking me how long I've been in Alaska; do I like it and so on? I know they all had to notice that for some reason I would not take it out of first gear. As I'm writing this, I'm sitting here laughing on how well I bluffed my way down the trail and acting as if I knew what I was doing. I truly did not know how to put it in second gear. The only thing that saved me was the fact that it was snow and ice on the trail so I had to go kind of slow. I'm sure after I took them to headquarters, they probably asked themselves, "Did he know what the hell he was doing?" When I got back to the motor pool, I immediately asked one of the mechanics where in the hell is second and third gear on this car, and he showed me. So now, I know how to drive a three-speed shift on the steering column.

CHAPTER 9

Land of the Midnight Sun

The two winters I had experienced in this region of the world were quite amazing to say the least, such as being so cold that you could visibly see the cold (ice fog), using the *inside* of our window seals in our room as a refrigerator, and actually not seeing the sun shine at all for approximately three months. Not to mention experiencing 85° below zero weather and that was *without* counting the wind chill factor. When the summer finally began to roll around, I was in for more spectacular and extraordinary events of nature. The enormous amount of snow accumulated does not melt, as we are accustomed to down in the states. It evaporates day by day by what is known as the *Chinook Winds* that come from the south and before you know it, day by day, you finally see dry land in a lot of places. The warmest temperature that I had experienced in the region I was in was around 80°. It wasn't hot, but a very pleasant and comfortable welcomed temperature compared to its winter counterpart. You see people walking around with short pants on taking advantage of this break, from the norm.

YOUR DECISIONS DETERMINE YOUR DESTINY

One bizarre thing about this short time of year, it does not get dark, at all. Unlike during the winter when we did see at least one and a half hours of heavy gray overcast each day, it wasn't much but at least it was some light. That's why this region is referred to as *The Land of the Midnight Sun*. That reference in of itself is an oxymoron. How can the sun be out at midnight? Let me try to explain it. Keep in mind that you are at the top of the globe. As the earth spins on its axis, and because you're located at the top of the globe, that simply means you experience a shorter rotation. When you are very close to the North Pole, the sun doesn't necessarily rise, but moves into position. And because it's a shorter earth circle to rotate, the sun seems to move over for a few hours and out of sight, and then move back quicker than normal because of your geographical position. So therefore, it really doesn't have time to get dark. You can say that in all actuality, one day lasts for three months. The sun will be shining around 11:30 PM to 12 and during this short peculiar season, they have midnight baseball games without any artificial light. In the barracks, we had to hang dark green army blankets over our window to keep the sun from shining in so we could go to sleep. Quite weird and took some getting used to.

During this time, we continued to get high, smoke marijuana and pop a bunch of pills. The landscape as well as the skies was some of the most breathtaking experiences that I have ever witnessed. I don't blame the Army for my choices, but it did give me the exposure and the experience with a lot of drugs, if nothing else. As noted earlier, the heroin use wasn't as prevalent, thank God. I would wander out in the wilderness at times high on acid or LSD and what was already a magnificently beautiful country, however, with the mind altering chemicals in my body it momentarily kept convincing me that I was on another planet and had left planet earth. Never seen anything like this before or since.

The soil in the short summer was quite fertile, producing unbelievable sizes of heads of lettuce like the size of a gym beach ball particularly in the Matanuska-Susitna Valley. Because the land was so dry, fires would sometimes start during the summer. And if they happened to be near any of the surrounding Eskimo villages, we would dispatch and go out and try to pick up any natives that would be threatened with any potential danger.

Land of the Midnight Sun

One of the strangest cultural practices that the Eskimos sometimes do (which I studied later years in a Sociology class), was the fact that if you do anything to help a family from any type of danger, it's their practice to offer you their wife for a night, and would consider it a great insult if you didn't oblige. Faced with this unusual dilemma, being that I was just 18 years old, I wanted a daughter, not a wife. No dice. I passed on that one, and made a decision to allow one of my buddies to oblige their custom graciously, and he did. You can't make this up, strange or not, you can say that taboo practices occur in many places, we have just never been exposed to or even heard about it.

Due to my crafty shenanigans when I was in the Headquarters office, I flew home on leave a few times and one of the times while I was at the Fairbanks Airport I almost got busted for trying to smuggle some marijuana and some pills on the plane. Alvin Leblanc of New Orleans and I made a decision to smoke a couple of joints in the bathroom of the airport. Right after we came out of the bathroom one of the workers went in right behind us. He immediately came back out with a very unhappy look on his face. Fortunately, for Alvin, his plane was leaving right away but my flight wasn't taking off for another 45 minutes. The worker right away went and informed a couple of security guys and then they proceeded to set a trap. I'm not in my uniform but in civilian clothes with this big fly hat on, zip up dress boots, flair bottom pants, and a short jacket with two ounces of weed condensed into one bag, with a few hits of speed on top of the grass. The time in the airport is late at night around 11 or 12. There aren't hardly any passengers in this small airport.

When security started looking around, guess who they set their sights on? Me! I'm starting to get a bit nervous but I wouldn't show it. I have a clear decision to make. That was easy because I'm getting on that plane and flying home. So the chair that I'm sitting in is a row of connected chairs. Directly right at the back of these chairs are some artificial plant boxes. When they took their eyes off me, I reached in my jacket pocket and slipped that big fat double-ounce bag of weed into the plant box behind me. I then got up and walked away in a cool manner putting some distance between it and me.

YOUR DECISIONS DETERMINE YOUR DESTINY

I'm sitting now at least about 50-75 feet away from that stash. The legs on the plant box stood at least three feet high under the plant box. From where I'm sitting now, I looked back that way and you could clearly and visibly see this fat bag of weed on the floor even from 75 feet away. I thought that I placed the weed in the plant box but it evidently fell through and hit the floor. When the security team noticed it on the floor, I was sitting back chillin'. They seemed to go into a frenzy probably thinking, "Oh we got him now." Looked like they were really getting worked up, but they would not touch it. They were waiting for me to retrieve it and attempt to board the plane.

"They must be crazy," I thought to myself, "if they think, I'm going anywhere near that stuff." I left there and boarded my plane upset with myself for letting Alvin talk me into smoking those joints in the bathroom. That was a close and scary call! I had to leave that stuff at the airport or get locked up. Easy decision.

One other time coming back off leave, by way of JFK airport in New York, I almost got busted again. What had happened was in the year of 1972, there were multiple plane hijackings and therefore customs began to tighten up their security. This upgrade happened while I was home on a 30-day leave. I'm thinking things are still relaxed in terms of leaving the states and was totally unaware of the recent security upgrades. When I walked around to the gate, once again not in my Army uniform, but instead wearing a big fly hat, hipster suede jacket, flair bottom pants, a pair of leather platform boots with the zipper on the side. I was flying but scared to death when I walked around to that gate and saw all those security officers that I hadn't seen before. Before all you had to do was just walk through the metal detector. Now, they pat you down for a thorough search. I had half an ounce of Colombian Gold weed inside one boot and the other half in the other boot. All of the seated passengers waiting to board the plane and the rest of the security team are watching everyone that's getting searched. At that moment, all eyes are on you. It was almost like you are in the spotlight on a Carnegie Hall stage. Although I was scared to death, you couldn't tell, I was as cool as a cucumber. The officer patted me from top to bottom, feeling basically my entire body. I was thinking to myself, "Aww man, I screwed up big time on this one." When

Land of the Midnight Sun

he got down to my boots, I swear he actually felt the marijuana and then told me to go have a seat with the rest of the passengers waiting to board the flight. I proceeded over with my little smooth swagger and took my seat. I was so happy I didn't know what to do. I promised myself that I would never do that again, but I broke my promise to myself and did do it again at a later time.

At this point with my time in the service, I had flown quite a few times. One time in particular was the craziest and dumbest thing I think I've ever done as a teenager. One of the times I was to come home on leave, I had to catch that Pan Am 747 flight that came from Japan, and stopped in Alaska to refuel and collect more passengers. It was an 8 to 9 hour non-stop flight from this point straight to New York JFK. It was customary that I, as well as most of my buddies got high before boarding the plane. I got hold of a piece of *LSD 25* from a buddy of mine, right before I boarded. He told me that it wasn't that strong, so why not. When we reach 35,000 feet in the air, after about half an hour had gone by, it hit me. Now I have experienced *tripping* off psychedelics many times before, but on the ground, not on a plane. I will never forget this experience as long as I live.

What happened was as I was looking out my window at the clouds, at some point the clouds began to look like a great big giant cotton, fluffy bed. One thing about when you're *tripping* off acid or LSD, or any hallucinogens, you either forget or don't realize that you are *tripping*. You're kind of in and out of reality at least that was always my experience. Anyone that has experienced this, you know what I'm talking about. Anyway, after staring at this big cotton bed outside of my window, and thinking how much fun it would be bouncing up and down in all of that cotton, I then began to look at the emergency door. I remember going back and forth. Looking out the window and looking at the handle on the emergency door. Thank God, I had a moment of sanity. I began to feel afraid of what I might do. Some of the moments I was briefly sane and momentarily in touch with reality and a lot of the moments I were literally out of my mind, and I couldn't control the duration of either one. Not even realizing, if I had opened that door, all of us would have been sucked right out of that cabin, me first.

YOUR DECISIONS DETERMINE YOUR DESTINY

I made a decision to confront a stewardess and warned her that I was not in my right mind. I'm sure that my dilated pupils and glassy eyes confirmed my confession. I requested that she and the other stewardess take turns sitting with me in the back of the plane until we landed. And that's exactly what happened. Thank God that I didn't make flight 914 a statistical air disaster. Today, it makes me understand perfectly, why young people, some of them anyway, are so dumb and crazy. I certainly was. Stationed in Alaska has left an affect on me that will last throughout my lifetime. Particularly how I view cold weather. To this day I underdress during the winter unless it gets (what we consider) brutally cold. My mind usually tells me it's just a little nippy when the weather drops below the freezing mark back home.

CHAPTER 10

From the Icebox to the Oven

———◆———

After completing my 18-month overseas tour of duty, which included two winters and one summer, I was ready to transfer to my next assignment. Alaska was considered overseas duty because we received Foreign Duty pay and Isolation pay. My next assignment was down in the lower 48's, (the way it is referred to in the Artic), at Fort Hood, Texas. I was sent home on leave back to Baltimore. Then I flew out to Texas. When I was in Alaska, I promised myself that I was not going to smuggle any more marijuana on the plane anymore. My excuse for doing so again was that I just simply love smoking pot. This time I packed an ounce in my suitcase, and not on my person like I foolishly did at JFK airport in New York, and attempted to do in Fairbanks, AK. When I arrived in Texas after spending two winters just below the Arctic Circle, it felt like I stepped into an oven. This was in the spring of 1973. Don't quite remember what the temperature was in Texas that day but whatever it was it felt

YOUR DECISIONS DETERMINE YOUR DESTINY

50° hotter to me. I thought for a minute that I couldn't handle that extreme weather transition. I remember saying to myself, "Do they think I'm a guinea pig or something?"

At first, I got assigned to a section called North Ft. Hood, maybe 25 to 30 miles from the main base. Hooked up with a *get high* buddy right away, he pulled out some weed straight from Mexico, and I pulled out the weed I brought in from Baltimore. After comparing the two, I threw mine in the trashcan. This post was set up in the boonies and there wasn't a lot to do. As usual, I smoked a lot of weed and a couple of occasions shot up some heroin that was also straight out of Mexico. They called it *Mexican Mud*. It doesn't take long for a promising drug addict to connect to his source. I recall one night when I was pulling my CQ duty; I had met a girl from a nearby town and snuck her into the barracks. We had some fun doing our thing; then almost got caught by the CO as he was doing his rounds. I've come to believe at that time that sneaking around, breaking rules, and defying authority was just the thing for me to do. After nearly two years in the US Army and all the trouble I got myself into up in Alaska, I still had main issues with complete compliance. I seemed to continue making decisions based on self-centered motives.

Eventually they moved me down to the main base and I began to interact and connect quite easily with the right crowd or some may call the *wrong crowd*. Getting high is what we mostly did in the Army practically throughout my three-year time in service. I hooked with a good friend from Fort Wayne, Indiana. His name was Willie Shaw. He had a nice Cutlass, Oldsmobile. At times, he would be working on his car outside the barracks. Removing the head gaskets, tightening the cylinders, etc. He obviously knew what he was doing because when he put it back together, you could barely hear the motor running. I believe that we had some great times traveling back and forth to Waco and other towns, doing the clubs, and doing some great parties. In fact, he had a girlfriend in Waco before I arrived there, and had the keys to her apartment so that we could come and go as we pleased. We not only smoked weed regularly, but the heroin use was getting more frequent, as well. Eventually I purchased my first car. It was a sky blue 69 Oldsmobile Toronado. I had my eight-track player under the seat and a case of eight tracks on the center of the front seat as an armrest. I started making trips to Waco on my own, *high as a satellite,* and only by the grace of God, I didn't crash.

I can recall different times when I nodded off behind the wheel and drifted onto the side of the road. It could have turned out a lot worse only by crossing the centerline into oncoming traffic. This was during the time when we had one of our biggest Nation-wide gas crunches. Gas station lines were ridiculously long and the speed limit on the highway went from 80 to 65 miles per hour, it seemed like overnight. I eventually encountered some axle issues with my car. The Latino Comrade that sold me the car attempted several times to fix it for me, (the mechanic he was supposed to be), to no avail, so I had to let it go after driving it about seven months. At first, I was very angry with this dude and pressured him on a daily basis. Of course, I had little to no knowledge about mechanics myself. I eventually surrendered and let it go.

My buddy Willie and I connected to a couple of other buddies that had already been there, and they showed us the action in other towns. Texas is a very big state with a lot of places spread out if you don't mind traveling a bit. Why not? It's not as if we had something special to do on our off time. I continued to get high and eventually I was addicted to heroin for the first time in my life. As a result, I caught hepatitis B, with my yellow eyes revealing the symptoms of jaundice. My Company Commander took a good look at me one morning after I came in the *Orderly Room* tripping over things and knocking stuff off his desk, ordered me to go to these counseling sessions that they had on base for drug addicts. Later, I would have to complete the sessions successfully before they would let me out of the Army.

They eventually kicked me out of that unit and moved me on the other side of the post. Fort Hood is one of the largest Army posts in the country with three major Divisions: *1st Calvary Division*; *2nd Armor Division*; and *(HHC) Headquarters & Headquarters Company*, the one I was in. Shortly before, they moved me out of my last Unit, an officer was found murdered in a dumpster in that area. I heard about it but didn't give it much thought until they moved me to my next unit. The First Sergeant of the new unit heard about that murder and since I just came from

YOUR DECISIONS DETERMINE YOUR DESTINY

there, he must have thought that I might have been in on it. Now I was already busted down to a Private E1, once again (my usual pattern). That false reputation preceded me to such a degree that (Top) First Sergeant gave me special privileges. He was actually afraid that I was capable of committing or being a part of a homicide. "Not this guy," I thought to myself. During certain details, he would give me a few men to supervise so that I didn't have to work. Like I just stated, I was only a Private E-1, the lowest grade there is, and I was eating it up.

My buddy Willie from Ft. Wayne, Indiana paid me a visit one day a couple of months later at the new unit they put me in. He had come from the other side of the Post with a little treat for me. They had assigned him to working in this salvage yard where they kept all the vehicles we were able to retrieve from Viet Nam before we completely pulled out, in this same year of 1973. He was in the back of a 2 ½ ton Personnel Carrier truck one hot day in that salvage yard, (the same type of 2 ½ ton that went dead on me in Alaska), and he stumbled upon 10" x 12" manila envelope stashed inside this truck. His sergeant in charge noticed that he had something and told him to bring it to him. My buddy just ran off with it unsure of its content but obviously had a feeling that it was something that came straight out of Vietnam. When the coast was clear for him, he discovered that it was about 10 nicely packed *Papasan* glass vials of heroin. My buddy Willie recognized them immediately because he came from Vietnam before being sent to Texas and he was just ready to ETS (separate) from the service. From what I understand, these vehicles had been sitting on this hot Texas lot for several months. You would think that the heroin would have gone bad. No chance! Surprisingly, it was just as strong as ever. He shared some of it with me and saved some to take back home to Indiana.

Texas is a very spread out state. I didn't see it all, but I did see a great part of it. Dallas was nice. Not only the clubs were popping but also we were able to get G.I discounts at some of the nicest hotels in Dallas. Big spacious rooms overlooking the city at a very cheap price for us. At one of them, I had a chance to meet the Ohio Players and the Spinners from a show they had done the night before. My boys and I shook their hands when we met them in the lobby. We hit the road and traveled as often as we could.

From the Icebox to the Oven

One of my buddies from New Orleans had his wife and an apartment off base. We used to ride out there and get high and kill some time. This same buddy had to go out on field duty for a while. One evening I'm at the barracks and someone tells me that this lady is outside asking for me. Didn't have a clue who it might be, so I went out to see who it is and it's my buddy's wife. I sat in the station wagon and asked her, "What's up?" She got right to the point. Said that she had some *rubbers* and we could go for a ride. I didn't think twice about it. I have been to their home a few times eating their food, getting high and having fun. I made the decision and told her I couldn't do it. She obviously didn't handle rejection well because when my buddy got back from the field and heard about it, she flipped the script and said it was me going after her. He believed *her* and told me not to come to their apartment anymore. I felt betrayed and I was very hurt. I did stand on a couple of values at this time and didn't budge. I told myself from then on, "The next time somebody else offers, I'm taking it." I soon got over the resentment and let it go.

Couple of my other buddies from New Orleans, Louisiana, which borders Texas from the East, took me over there and as usual, we had some great times. Being a G.I. for me meant one thing and one thing only, fun. I caught the tail end of the Mardi Gras that year in New Orleans and it was one hell of an experience. I didn't want to leave, the possibilities were unlimited. Although I was in the Army, with civilian clothes on we blended right in and went with the flow, and it was good. I recall another Louisiana buddy of mine taking me to a town called New Iberia. He just came in from Germany and purchased a brand new Monte Carlo. We went to these girls' house out in the country that he already knew to take a couple of them out for fun. There were three or four sisters there and they knew only two of them were going with us, so they kind of auditioned a little, you might say. I couldn't wait to get out of there. But it turned out to be a very exciting night. We went dancing and got our separate rooms that night. Sometimes when we went to Louisiana, we didn't always make it back in time for Monday morning formation.

One of my two girlfriends that I left back home wanted to come visit me. Actually, she wanted to come visit me up in Alaska. I told her that you really don't want to do that. So I did allow her to fly down from

YOUR DECISIONS DETERMINE YOUR DESTINY

Baltimore to Texas. My car had gone up on me and an Italian buddy of mine let me borrow his brand new Chevy Impala for a few days. I thought that was big of him to do that for me. That was very unselfish of this guy. I got a motel room off base, she stayed about five or six days, and didn't want to leave. Informing me that she could get a job at the Holiday Inn because she had already worked at one back in Baltimore. At that time, I was not ready for or capable of that type of commitment. So I put her on a plane and sent her back home, amidst her strong protests. This same one had tried to keep me from boarding the bus to go into the Army.

My time is drawing near to separate from the service. They allowed you to choose from a list of available skills that you could learn in an effort to transition you back in society by a program called *Project Transition*. Other than driving, most of the jobs I seemed to have had were strictly military. We had an EM (Enlisted Man) nightclub on the base as well as an Offices Club on the base. The skill I chose was Club Manager; don't ask me why it just sounded like a smooth thing to do at the time. Actually, it was just a get over so I could have in easy ride on my way out. A good buddy of mine from Kansas City, along with his wife was staying two miles off post in a little town called Killeen. His wife was pregnant and decided to return home to have the baby. While she was gone, he invited this white girl by the name of Marilyn to stay with him. I had partied a little with them both at his place, a time, or two. For some reason, he had to return to Kansas City temporarily also. I received a message in the Unit Office to give Marilyn a call. I called back and then shortly made the decision and went to the place where she was, his place. This is definitely not like the last situation, I reasoned within myself. I'm taking this one! I wound up staying there for perhaps a week.

I recall she had this boa constrictor pet snake and when I tried to hold him he began to pull away and I fearfully, let him go. It was the first time that I ever picked up a snake of that size. His body felt like one long muscle. Anyway, one day she and I were walking to the store. By this time, I'm still without a car and I never got another one. Using became my primary focus so I just wasn't motivated to get another car. As we were walking, I recall maybe about three or four hillbillies riding past in a pickup truck saying "Hey nigger, what you doing?"

From the Icebox to the Oven

Marilyn was saying quietly under her breath, "Please don't say anything." Although I have never in my life been called that to my face, I realized, I was in the Deep South. By the way, when I first got down there they told me what Killeen stood for. (K-ill e-ach and e-very n-igger), I remembered that and kept it moving. I was becoming real short, as we called it (little time left), and I still had to be clean and off drugs to get out. It's amazing what you can do when you have the right motivation behind you. I made the decision to get clean, but only for that purpose and separated from the US Army with an Honorable Discharge by the hair of my *chinny chin chin*. This was July 11, 1974. I completed exactly three years of service at 20 years of age, and now on my way back to Baltimore.

CHAPTER 11
Back to Reality

As I returned to Baltimore with certain wounds and scars that weren't apparent right away, the process of coming back home was not an easy transition. I didn't quite know what to expect. I truly didn't have an idea of what I really wanted to do, and my experience with getting high in the Army qualified me to be a certified and bona fide drug addict, once I was finally separated from that man's Army. Although I managed to get off the heroin temporarily, as I was required to do, to get out of the Army, the seed of addiction was securely planted. I moved back with my mother and father in West Baltimore and began transition back into civilian life, this time as an adult. I left home as a 17-year-old teenager and obviously returned back home as a 20-year-old *teenager*. Some things that I had learned and the many experiences I was exposed to were mostly filtered through the lens of drinking and drugging. I refer to getting high as repetitiously as I do because that particular behavior dominated the theme of my experience the majority of my time away.

Those three years did have a profound effect on me, however, not so much in a positive manner as one would expect. I wasn't in a big hurry to

YOUR DECISIONS DETERMINE YOUR DESTINY

find employment when I arrived back to the *real world*, let alone decide on a career path. However, I didn't have a problem connecting with my buddies and getting high every day. I became used to doing this activity on a daily basis. In the first year I was home, I kind of just squandered my time. Because I was a recently returning veteran, my mother suggested that I apply for a job at the Social Security Administration in downtown Baltimore. I followed her suggestion. To my surprise, I got hired. I worked up on the sixth floor with a lot of other people doing pretty much the same type of clerical work. It became boring pretty fast, however, there were a bunch of pretty ladies in the building.

My one girlfriend at the time had just brought a brand-new Grenada, but she didn't have a driver's license yet. Therefore, for a good while, I drove her car back and forth to work even though we didn't live together. Just entering my twenties, I was still somewhat shy when it came to the ladies, but just like when I was in high school, (let me tell it), I was God's gift to the ladies. Needless to say, at this time I had more than two or three relationships. This was the year of 1975 and a year before the 1976 Olympics. Right across the street from my job was the Baltimore Civic Center, and I recall at times during my lunch break walking across the street and watching Sugar Ray Leonard prepare for the Olympics. Early on, I began to understand the concept of supply and demand. In this government building I'm working in, I happened to notice that there were plenty of pot smokers willing to purchase some good weed if it were conveniently accessible. I had contacts and I had suppliers.

To enter this government building at any time of day you have to walk through a metal detector, and that was for everyone. I decided to smuggle in nearly a pound of marijuana broken down into packages of ounces, half ounces, $10 bags, and what was popularly known as nickel ($5) bags. As I entered the building standing in line with everyone else first thing in the morning, I would have all of this marijuana taped on my person and evenly distributed so as not to reveal any suspicious irregularities. Yes, I was a bit concerned with getting caught because once again, I'm gambling with Federal charges to say the least. No problem, every time. Then I would board the elevator and head up to my floor. Once on the floor, I would proceed to the men's bathroom and stand on

Back to Reality

the toilet seat and lift up one of the ceiling tiles, and stash my drugs. Whenever someone wanted to *cop*, either from my floor or whatever floor was requesting, I would go and inconspicuously retrieve whatever package they requested. So I'm a little big shot in a government building.

Just like back up in Alaska, I foolishly had no respect or fear of the government. I was smoking weed regularly and every now and then shooting up some heroin. I evidently wasn't taking this job too serious. I would flirt and kiss a couple of ladies, (of course not at the same time), behind the tall file cabinets. Sometimes I would catch myself nodding a little at my desk. I recall a coworker or two, walking by, shaking me, and them warning me to cool it, as I kept dipping into a *nod*. I recall a work evaluation that my supervisor gave me wasn't too good, understandably so. I was there physically for the most part and that was it. In fact, he was threatening to fire me if I didn't shape up. One day sitting at my desk on the open floor, I noticed the supervisor rushing to the bathroom and then coming out feverishly looking around. I asked, "What's going on?" Someone said they found a bunch of marijuana in the bathroom. Naturally, I played it cool as a cucumber, but I had mixed feelings. I was naturally upset of losing that stash but more than grateful that I didn't get a charge for it, especially in a government building. Some of the chances I took were obviously not governed by sound decisions. They obviously removed the drugs out of there and to my knowledge, didn't have any clear suspects. That ended my weed business in the Social Security Administration downtown building.

Eventually my supervisor called me in for an updated evaluation. It was not good. He said, due to your poor performance and no apparent improvement, we would have to terminate your employment. I was there about one year at this point. Prior to this expected termination, I managed to get close to a couple of the ladies I worked with. Close like going to each of their houses and *getting busy*. One of them in particular, Venus McDowell, was a member of the Credit Union because she had been there for at least a couple of years. The credit union there often gave trips abroad for a very attractive price, but you have to be a member of the credit union. They offered a trip to the Bahamas for seven days at a cost of $229 per person. This took care of the airfare and the resort. You only

YOUR DECISIONS DETERMINE YOUR DESTINY

had to provide food for yourself. Although Venus had never flown before, I talked her into going. I would go as her husband. So we booked the trip.

I ran into an uncle of mine that gave me an ounce of Colombian Gold Marijuana. *Here I go again.* So I go to the drugstore and purchase a jar of Blue Magic hair grease. I took the top off of the jar, I took a tablespoon, dug down into the center of the jar, and removed a great amount of its content. Then I carefully folded the ounce of this exotic Colombian Gold and inserted it into the middle of the jar. I then put back the amount of grease that I took out and smoothed the top with the spoon. Then the finishing touches were to take a lit match and tilt the jar slightly upside down and melt the top layer as if it has never been tampered with. Held the jar up to the light to see if I could see any of its hidden contents and I couldn't. So I tossed it in the suitcase and we took off.

When we landed in Nassau, Bahamas, we naturally had to go through customs. I remember at the airport that we were greeted with a warm melody as they were playing their Calypso music creating and maintaining the Caribbean atmosphere. This would be my first trip to the Caribbean and right away, I felt real good landing on this exotic island. I was feeling the groove of the music right up until I'm standing in line as the custom agents are checking the bags of the passengers in front of me, on this long table. Now reality begin to set in. Right away, there was an issue with my identification. My driver's license stated my real name of Steven Middleton. But the name on the trip documents stated Steven McDowell. Remember, the only way that I would be able to go on this trip would be posing as Venus's husband. I simply explained the confusion to the Custom Agent that the only chance I had to visit this beautiful island was to pose as this pretty lady's husband. Could you blame me? He said I understand, go ahead. Okay, now for the weed check. *Here I go again,* asking myself, "What is wrong with me? Why do I keep making these wacky decisions tempting fate and threatening my freedom?"

I realized later that bringing weed to the Caribbean is like bringing sand to the beach, it is already there. They opened my suitcase, my heart beating like a bongo drum, but you couldn't tell by the cool look that I've learned to put on my face from previous insane decisions. The agent

Back to Reality

actually picked up the jar of the Blue Magic hair grease, looked at it briefly and tossed it back in the suitcase saying, "Go ahead." I was so happy and relieved. I must have gotten off on some kind adrenalin kick with this weed and airport thing! I can't figure it out. When we got to our hotel room, I immediately retrieved my weed and we started smoking. Outright defiance definitely played a part.

After this first trip abroad to the islands, decisions would decree that I would not be able to get back there until nearly 30 years later. My friend and I at 20 years old had a fantastic experience on that island. We swam in the pool, walked along the beach shore at night like the one you would see in a movie. The American candy tasted real funny there as if some sea-salted air affected it when it was transported over. Making that decision to go there would prove to be one of my few smart decisions I would make as a young man. Many couples for whatever reason decide not to experience such an exotic getaway, much less than at 20 years old. I brought back a couple of small gifts one in particular being a 50 cent bill. When we returned home, I didn't have a job anymore, but I had a great time going out.

CHAPTER 12
Where to from Here?

After coming back from my little paradise trip, I still found myself confronted with life on life's terms. Still getting high seemed to be the theme of my life. I need to point this ever-present reality out because it helps to establish the track that I'm clearly on and where this train is unavoidably headed. The fact that a lot of people around me are doing the same easily allows me to justify and rationalize being irresponsible. Now in my 20s, I'm still having difficulty in grasping the concept of being a productive citizen in society. Could it be the drugs? Certainly, not everyone is necessarily a product of their environment; however, *those* that are *not* are probably the exception rather than the rule. The many dynamics that come into play influencing a young African-American's decisions are probably distinctive as the individual himself. Looking from the outside of the window seems always to entice one to impose their standards on how a person should think and behave. But when you are actually in *those* shoes and influenced by the different

YOUR DECISIONS DETERMINE YOUR DESTINY

factors that affect *you*, things all of a sudden appear quite different. It's very difficult to respect or understand an experience that you cannot personally relate to or identify with.

Then there is always that *Grand Design* that yourself, and people that are close to you are completely oblivious to. In other words, despite the sometimes-dangerous decisions, one can make, despite the obvious irresponsible posture that one can maintain, and even the very clear misguided path one is on, it all can very possibly play a very strategic and divinely orchestrated role in guiding a person to the destiny that awaits them. Who is to say that it can't be? If we agree that who we are in the present is mostly determined by the experiences we encountered along the way, then there shouldn't be a problem adopting the perspective that I just presented. I attempted a couple of jobs here and there and without any commitment at either place. My times of employment were very limited. Again, attempting to follow the example of my brother Poochie in the same way as I did going into the Army and acquiring a veteran status, I decided to attend a community college under the G.I. Bill.

During my exposure to the higher learning atmosphere was a bit challenging and intimidating, probably because my heart or passion just weren't there. My motivation for returning to school was misplaced and well over thirty years later, I would again act on the same misplaced motives but the second time with a deeper and far-reaching outcome. I'll explain in a later chapter. The VA sent a check to my house every month for attending school. For the most part, I was there physically, but my mind at the time just wouldn't grasping the reality that I signed up for. The classes just seemed to be too much work that I was not willing to commit to.

However, my sociology class was particularly interesting, especially when we were discussing various cultures around the world. One in particular we discussed was the Eskimo custom of offering their wife after receiving a service rendered to them. I felt real good sharing the fact that while I was stationed in Alaska I had the opportunity to experience that particular custom. I witnessed it in action perhaps 4-5 years prior to me taking that class. I think the class was a little impressed with my

Where to from Here?

eyewitness account of that practice and that seemed to be the highlight of my academic attempt. Except when my psychology teacher at one time asked me did I want to teach the class since I obviously projected a bit of arrogance by *acting as if* I knew everything. Can you imagine that?

I was still receiving a check from the VA for going to school although I had made the decision to stop attending, shortly after signing up. Although the benefit of completing would have been very rewarding and probably the very thing I needed to do, I just wasn't *feeling it*. The checks continued to come to my house and I continued foolishly to cash them. Until I received a letter from the VA, stating this is the total that you need to pay back. So much for easy money that I thought, I was getting. This debt would pose as a stumbling block nearly 20 years down the road when I attempted to purchase my home.

I still needed to earn some income and begin to contribute towards the welfare of my existence. On my mother's side of my family, I had two uncles that operated a very successful Auto Reconditioning business. This location was out in the county and each and every one of the boys in our extended family spent some time learning how to detail used automobiles. The founder of the business and a true pioneer was my uncle Jesse. He and I had a few things in common. Like him, I didn't have any children at this time. We were both the youngest in the family, and we were both born in the very same house that belonged to my grandparents. Not to leave out, we were both prone to the very same disease known as addiction.

Jesse was so sharp with his game, that in his twenty's when he went into business for himself, he was easy making a couple of thousands of dollars for himself and paying workers on a weekly basis. The backdrop of time was the early 1960's. He was making more money than doctors were making at this time in his life. Had it not been for the disease of addiction, he would have been a very wealthy man. He took me under his wing for quite some time. I don't know, perhaps because he had no children of his own and we *clicked* into a nice chemistry. He wanted to instill a lot of the expertise and knowledge that led him to be successful and establish a reputable name in that business. He taught me to see things not as they are, but as they could be.

YOUR DECISIONS DETERMINE YOUR DESTINY

We moved around a lot on a mobile basis visiting many of the car dealerships. We went out to some car dealers in the summer and for lunch; the manager would grill steaks in back of the car lot. My uncle was smooth and knew how to develop and cultivate relationships in a business sense, unlike I had ever seen before. Even to a used tractor-trailer dealership, that had a fleet of up to 75 tractor-trailer's cabs, side by side on the lot. We shampooed and polished just the interior, of each and every cab on that lot. Sometimes he would leave me by myself to get the job done and I did because he trained me well. One day the manager that gave him the contract approached me when I was working alone. He then propositioned me to perhaps consider taking on another negotiated contract cutting my uncle out of the picture. I immediately refused to stab Jesse in the back. He just wasn't teaching me how to make money, but he was also my mother's youngest brother. In other words, family.

As a result of the progression of Jesse's addiction, the base operation of the business was left to be run by one of his brothers, uncle JP. JP as well took the business to another level. The two of them made so much money for reconditioning cars like you wouldn't believe. Initially that was their exclusive source of income until they later invested in property and other enterprises. We all were very proud of our uncles. Later Jesse and I decided to take a trip to Florida.

In the meantime, the work was not year round but seasonal. Off-season I basically did nothing but hang out with a girlfriend and yes, continue to get high on a regular basis. Did I forget to mention that Uncle Jesse and I smoked weed each and every day that we worked. I had moved out from my parent's house at one point and moved in with a girlfriend by the name of Anita that had a house left to her by her grandmother by the age of 18. (Still seeking a soft and easy way or a shortcut). She was a very nice young lady, loving, caring, and giving. Although there was no rent to be paid, we still need to eat and pay a couple of other bills. I tried a job in between cleaning cars at a wholesale bakery but was unable to commit. The few little dollars that I did decide to share with her was insulting, to say the least. As nice a young lady as she was, everyone has a breaking point. She kindly let me know either bring in or leave out. I wasn't contributing to the house in no significant way, but surely smoking

Where to from Here?

my weed daily and even got my hands on a little cheap weightlifting set and set it up in her house. I kind of hated to give up a sweet *get over*, but evidently it ran its course and so I did her a great big favor, and left. Had another girlfriend on the side anyway but the thing was that she didn't have her own place, like myself.

One of my cousins, Warren had moved out to California and was in town with his girlfriend visiting his mother. We spent some time together as kids; in fact, one of the stops during my *Summer Tours* chapter was at his home. More correctly put, my Uncle Jimmy's house, my mother's oldest brother. Warren invited me go back out California with them when they were to leave. I said why not and made the decision to go. We boarded a plane (no drugs this time) I don't think, flew to Texas, and picked up his car. Then drove from Texas through New Mexico and Arizona into California.

We stopped one night in a little town called Portales, New Mexico where his girlfriend's sister lived. She wanted to move to California and rode with us. Before we left Portales, we drank some corn liquor by the name of *White Lightening*. It was believed to be 190 proof. I swear I thought I was drinking liquid fire. We took off in his 1977 Thunderbird. As we were making our way through the *Mojave Desert* in Arizona, the heat outside was around 110 Degrees. The air conditioning inside the car was doing us little good during that long stretch of highway. As we seemingly came down into the valley of California, you could clearly see the smog in the air. It was no wonder they had *smog alert* days at times when it was heavy.

This was my first time going to Cali with a bunch of preconceived notions. Truth of the matter was, I really didn't know what to expect or even what was the real reason for me deciding to go out there. I stayed out there for a few months and nothing really spectacular occurred. We drank and smoked weed every day. I looked for work but never obtained any probably because in the back of my mind, I was just visiting. I had the opportunity to work at a wine refinery, but turned it down. I did join the gym out there. I had started an interest in working out back in Bmore, despite my ongoing use of drugs and alcohol. I brought a little sand coated

YOUR DECISIONS DETERMINE YOUR DESTINY

weight set and a bench. What really motivated me was the natural 8-pack I had. Because I was skinny and a little athletic at the time, I had an 8-pack that you could see from across the street with a shirt on, for real.

We went to LA and we visited the Grauman's Chinese Theater where the movie stars have their footprints and handprints on the ground. We also visited Magic Mountain amusement park. I met this one girl out there that was very nice, it just didn't go anywhere. This stay lasted about four months and this one girlfriend I left back home was on my mind. Not too sure, why I decided to go out there in the first place. Something to do I guess.

Time for me to head back east so I decided to allow the Welfare Agency to send me back on a Trailways bus. I recall two of the older ladies that worked at the agency telling me, "We should take you home with us instead of giving you this bus ticket." I believe they were serious. My decision was already made. I promised myself I would never, ever ride a bus that long ever again, and I haven't. We left Upland, California Tuesday night at 11:30 PM. We arrived in Baltimore that Saturday afternoon. Naturally making a lot of stops for people getting on and getting off along the way. Almost came close to allowing this woman to talk me into going on with her to Indiana. Didn't know her from a can of paint but after few smooches in the back of the bus when it was dark, it kind of sounded like a nice idea. I did in fact notice one or two guys hooking up and going home with a couple of the ladies. Hopefully, they made out.

CHAPTER 13
A Chance of a Lifetime

It seems like when I came back from Cali, I pretty much resumed my irresponsible and unproductive lifestyle. Back to staying in my parent's basement, I continued to get high and clean a few cars here and there. I actually moved my little sand covered weightlifting set and bench, back to my parent's basement. This was around the time I wanted seriously to build my body up, having wanted to do that since I was that eight and nine-year-old kid in the Cherry Hill projects. Only thing, I was convinced that when I smoked a joint before a work out, it would be a more productive workout. So I got into the routine of getting high off marijuana before I worked out. Always looking for an excuse to justify my getting high, I got high off weed before I did any kind of work. I got high first thing in the morning, I got high last thing at night, and I think you have the picture. When I was able to reach a minimum of success, it seemed like I would reach back time and time again picking up that heroin and losing the ground I

YOUR DECISIONS DETERMINE YOUR DESTINY

had previously gained. It appeared that I was incapable to stop and seriously ponder the thought, could it be the drugs?

Even if I were able to admit partially to the fact that drugs were ruining my life, I just couldn't see living without them in my life. So, despite all of the overwhelming evidence that everyone could plainly see, I remained locked and loaded into a comfortable space called denial. I was getting pretty much sick of my lifestyle, and so were my parents. When we both had reached our wits end, I would go into a rehab, basically for a temporary break. I need to be clear about the fact that most of my previous attempts to get off drugs were always half-hearted and I was just going through the motions. I realize now you have to get truly sick and tired of your ways, then you will become willing to take the necessary steps. Unfortunately, I was far from that point. Even after a couple of more rehabs. Good thing I was a Veteran or I wouldn't have had access to the help, that I obviously didn't take completely advantage of.

One of the very wealthy car dealer owner's, asked my uncle **Jesse** to travel down to Naples, Florida to straighten out and fix up a used car dealership down there. This particular dealer by the name of Bill Schaefer owned a couple of lucrative new car dealerships in Maryland and had been successful for quite some time. My uncle Jesse had a real tight relationship with this guy as well as others. He shared with me, "I knew this guy when he had one small used car lot." Now he's a multi-millionaire and Jesse also partially shared with me that Mr. Shafer engaged in some unscrupulous practices as he was rising to the top. When he asked Jesse to travel to Florida, Jesse then asked me to go with him. I really didn't have anything going on at home at the time; therefore, I made a decision to ride out. We loaded up and jumped into his 1978 Chrysler. He and I smoked our weed during the whole trip. We took turns driving. He would drink a little Vodka here and there in which I had no interest to partake in. I guess we were trying to make the trip as enjoyable as possible.

When we arrived in Naples, the weather was quite hot compared to the winter in Baltimore. We both were dressed for the cold winter up North, but when we reached the 80 + degrees in Southern Florida, we shed a lot of clothes real fast. We pulled up on Schaefer's car lot

A Chance of a Lifetime

and assessed the situation. Partly why this guy was probably successful is that he obviously knew when to make the right decisions for the right situation. In other words, instead of hiring local Recon and detail professionals, he chose to import the top talent that he was keenly aware of. Next, we had to find a place to stay. We first tried a little efficiency for a few days, but it was too expensive and too small. Then Mr. Schaefer suggested that we stay with a friend of one of his maids. We did and it worked out for a while.

Meanwhile back on the car lot, we simonized and detailed at least 50 to 75 cars. Then we assembled them on the frontline of the lot in a color-coded rainbow fashion. It was a work of art. My uncle Jesse was one of the best in the business and Mr. Schaefer knew this. Naples was a money town. There were good opportunities to make good money there. This is how much of a confident and relaxed type of a relationship that my uncle had with this wealthy man. I have seen my uncle Jesse walk into Mr. Schaefer's office when he was in town, and Mr. Schaefer would have a pair of expensive solid gold frame sunglasses sitting on his desk and Jesse would say, "Hey Schaf, I dig them man, let me have them." And without hesitation, he handed them right to him. One of the things that I really admired about my uncle is that he knew what he wanted, and wasn't ashamed to go after it. Jesse and I were then invited to his 2 1/2 million dollar Florida home, with this $300,000 speedboat parked out back on his private pier. We're sitting up in there drinking beer and kicking it.

I'm saying to myself, "This is *A Chance of a Lifetime.*"

Back where Jesse and I were renting this room, and a very nice and clean room it was with two single beds and access to the kitchen, we come to find out that this woman was a very religious woman. She lived alone except with a young daughter around the age of 10 years old. At times on a weekly basis, she would invite her church sisters over and they would have I guess you would say a worship service in the living room. It sounded real strange to Jesse and me when we couldn't help but listen to their particular style of worship. Now with Jesse and me coming in there I'm sure *high* off one thing or another, it really sounded

YOUR DECISIONS DETERMINE YOUR DESTINY

a bit creepy out there. We would look at each other in our room with that distinctive frown on our faces that depicts, "What the hell is going on out there?" We heard sounds of groaning and wailing, speaking in tongues and such. I guess you would almost believe that you were listening to a *cult* of some type.

We are in fact deep down in Florida. Although we never smoked weed in her home, late at night when she was asleep and Jesse was asleep, I would sneak a girl up in there. This same girl, Helen Ann, introduced me to where the real drugs were. During our very first encounter, she burned me out of $20. I ran back into her later that evening and convinced her to get in the car with me. Naturally she did reluctantly not knowing exactly how I would come off on her for ripping me off of my money. I figured that since I'm new in town, I decided to let that $20 bucks go and focus more on connecting with others, through her. It was a short-lived relationship of course. Motivated by sex and dominated by drugs. She not only burned me for that little bit of money, but making the decision to *not* be responsible, she also wound up burning me with the *clap* (gonorrhea). Ouch! I had to go take care of that right away.

As time went on, perhaps three months later, Jesse decided to go back to Baltimore, his work was done, and I decided to remain there. I was loving this new lifestyle. Working for Mr. Schaefer as an independent contractor was cool, until he offered me to work on the clock and at that point, we parted ways. Mr. Schaefer's manager must have thought that since Jesse returned to Baltimore and I remained, that I would be happy with just a job. Wrong! I was trained very well by my uncle in that profession; and how to get money. So I began to do my own thing and was very successful in the beginning. I moved out of that lady's house, (cramped my style) and moved in with another girlfriend by the name of Kelly Rose. She had an apartment with two small kids. My mind was not on *putting it in park* with this woman, but just going with the flow: chasing money and chasing drugs. I noticed these Naples girls go by two names.

The mosquitoes were vicious, all throughout the day. I purchased a 1969 Chevrolet Impala that was in good condition. I then rented a buffer

A Chance of a Lifetime

machine but I had to get this local guy to sign it out for me since I was a visitor. I was literally a detail shop on wheels. I had everything I needed in the trunk of my car. I would pull up to different car dealerships, set up, and go to work. I quickly began to establish a name for myself with the artwork I could do with a used auto. Not only with commercial dealers, but also with private residential customers as well. Even at night on the outside, I would set up a spotlight and Recon a car or a pickup truck with precision, noticing people up on their balconies watching me do my thing. I repeat, I was trained by the best.

During this process I began to fool around with that cocaine more than I'd ever done before. I was making a lot of quick money and the cocaine was so plentiful and cheap. This particular drug was never *my drug of choice,* until I landed in Naples. Before Jesse had left, I had joined a gym and was working out early in the morning before work. I had even talked Jesse into joining the gym and he showed up for a hot minute, but that just wasn't his thing. I think my man lasted about two days and then I eventually stopped going myself, when working out became less of a priority and the drugs became more of a demand. Some things just don't go together. It seemed the more money I made, the more drugs I consumed. Here I have a great opportunity, *A Chance of a Lifetime*, but I can't shake loose this growing drug addiction.

As I continue to professionally clean and detail cars, I developed a stronger reputation and the word was being passed around. Unfortunately, I had a little secret. I'm still getting high on a daily basis and my using is clearly increasing. I would keep so much money on me at times that when I got high with people some of them really thought that I was the police or an undercover Narcotics Agent. Me? Really! I guess it was hard for them to conceive a young guy in my upper 20s doing what I was doing in this small town.

Word had got to a very successful businessman that I could recondition a vehicle like you wouldn't believe. His name was Frank and he owned and operated a business of installing outside swimming pools in the ground. In fact, he actually came to the area where I was staying seeking me out. He found me and invited me back to his place. I

YOUR DECISIONS DETERMINE YOUR DESTINY

followed him back out to his place, a modest home out in the suburbs and of course, with his own outside built-in swimming pool, equipped with a screen enclosure. I would do just a little needed work to his vehicles (take a damp sponge and wipe the dust from the interior of the car), and he would pay me around $100 for not even quite an hour. I realized then that when make a good name for yourself and the right people take a liking to you, money is not an object.

This guy liked the fact that I was a young hustler putting my thing down. So much to the point that he invited me and a friend of mine that told him about me into his home, drinking beer and *chewing the fat*. This guy was undoubtedly rich when he shared with us the many contracts he does on a regular basis. He had quickly acquired enough confidence in me that he had actually set up a business for me 20 miles south down in the *Everglades*. Where I would be making some ridiculous money. I have heard it said before that, *there is plenty room at the top*. The challenge is are you sure enough ready and want it bad enough. I remember going down there and I just now started laughing to myself. Those mosquitoes down there probably coming out of the swamps were so ferocious and were biting me so much that I would buff out an entire car in less than 15 minutes. This was early in the morning. I was good, but I never moved so fast buffing a car in my entire life. I thought I gave it a good shot; however, I had to pass. I made it back to Naples and my addiction continued to progress. Here I have once again a fantastic, *Chance of a Lifetime*, and I blew it. I realize what good is it to have a great opportunity, and not be mentally and spiritually prepared for it. In other words, *"Better to be prepared and not have the opportunity rather than have the opportunity and not be prepared."* Could it be the drugs? I was *cool* with not just one, but two different very rich guys that were impressed with my skills.

Things started going downhill pretty fast at this point. I had moved out of my girlfriend's house and was sleeping here and there, sometimes in my car. It got bad. The one rich guy Frank was taking his family on vacation. The friend of mine that introduced us who also by the way worked for this guy and was making great money during this time, came up with the idea to rob his house when he left to go on vacation. Yes, my friend was on drugs also. I decided that (I was in) despite all that this guy

A Chance of a Lifetime

tried to do for me. Drug use doesn't care about gratitude or appreciation. So we planned to go into the pool enclosure area where we knew he had a window slightly cracked with electric cord running out of it.

On the morning of him and his family departure, my buddy and I got into position. Just before we were about to open the door to the pool enclosure, his neighbors came over to use his swimming pool more than likely with his permission doing his absence. Stopped us in our tracks. That perfect timing had to be a God send. I began to decline almost as fast as I ascended. In a time frame of just a few months later, I not only was sleeping in my car, but also at times in a hotel room. I couldn't believe how fast I went down. When I checked out, I would leave the hotel room with the window unlocked. After they cleaned the room, sneak back in there and *crash*. I recall one of the nights I was in there; someone came with a door key and attempted to unlock the door. I had the chain on the door and I can hear them saying, "Someone is in there." When they went back to the lobby manager, I made my escape. I also left the window unlocked at times so I could sneak back in and steal the television sets. This is how low my addiction had brought me. One minute, I was at the top of my game and all the respect that went with it, the next minute feeling so low that I could shake hands with an insect. This is not why I came to Florida. My problem was not that "I aimed too high and missed, but aimed too low and hit." Time to get up out of here, before I perish.

Now before I could make my exit out of town, the guy that I had got to rent that buffer machine was trying to catch up with me. I never went back and made things straight with this guy. He was a little pissed off at me for using him as I did and not giving him any money as I promised. The community that I mostly stayed in set back on the other side of these railroad tracks. There is only one way in and one way out. He obviously heard of my soon departure and got into position to wait for me heading out. When we met up, he expressed his justifiable anger with me and demanded some kind of money. I'm sitting in my car and he is standing by the window on my driver's side. I had a few dollars out on my seat but I also had this fish scale knife in my right hand that he couldn't see. Decision time. I decided to go ahead and pay him some of what I owed him and kept the knife out of sight. I soon sold my car and hitchhiked a ride up the highway to Baltimore. Thinking to myself, wow, what a trip.

CHAPTER 14
I Just Didn't Know

Departing out of Florida was a very narrow escape. Right up until the day that I left, there could have very easily been some blood spilled. Perhaps his or maybe my own. I thank God that encounter didn't go the way that it could have easily went. I took advantage of some people as well as cheated some people out of their money. It had gotten that bad. As great as the opportunities that were before me, I had to surrender and accept the fact that I just wasn't ready. What that trip also revealed to me on the positive side was that when you are given the right opportunity, and you have the skills to make things happen, success will be looking you right in the eye. Provided that you are not stuck or imprisoned with a self-inflicted lifestyle. It also reinforced the belief of it's not where you're located or who your with, but the critical decisions that you make at that time.

More than one time I would ride from one job to another job in Florida with tears flowing out of my eyes. Faced and hurting with the realization of so much spiritual pain. I just didn't know how to stop using. Despite the great possibilities that were there in front of me, literally inviting

YOUR DECISIONS DETERMINE YOUR DESTINY

me to go to the next level, I just couldn't stop. I just didn't know what exactly I was up against spiritually and was clueless about the need for the process of recovery. I made that decision to let my car go just before my departure and I shouldn't have. I could have least came back home with my own transportation that would have possibly opened up different opportunities for me.

Decisions that are made from a desperate condition usually will result in regret. I was feeling a sense of defeat and at the same time a sense of relief. I regretted how that experience turned out and at the same time was glad and grateful I got away in one piece. Besides, I wasn't sure if the car would have made it up the road. Although I didn't have any other cars, I just couldn't see myself driving into town with an old Chevy. Don't look like I was thinking too straight. It became apparently clear that I had come to the end of the road in this little small money town and whether I was able to admit it or not, complete defeat was at hand. Stayed nearly a year in the town of Naples and all I had to show for it was an empty, torn person that just wanted to escape that reality and give it a try back home, once again.

I had made some empty promises to my girlfriend back home and was supposed to send for her to visit me while I was in Florida. As described in the previous chapter, that wasn't happening because of the mess, I was in, to her great disappointment. The idea of it was sincere at first in the beginning, until I landed in Florida where the drugs were so plentiful and allowed myself to get caught up, revealing the fact that my lack of control was completely out of hand. Despite the *once in a lifetime* opportunities I was fortunately presented, I really didn't have a chance. It's next to impossible to manage a business when you are completely out of control, not to mention keeping any promises. I was able to come back to my senses for a time when I made it back to my parent's basement. When I first appeared back on the block, my little niece Tasha was playing down the street. She was around 9 years old at the time. When she seen me back in town, she bolted toward me with so much excitement and delight jumping on me almost knocking me down. That made me feel so good at a time when I was almost convinced that I was nothing but a loser. I love my Tasha. Started working out again with my little start-up set and

I Just Didn't Know

began to see some noticeable improvement. I guess you can call me the *bounce back kid*. Just like when I used to drag myself into those rehabs weighing only 135 lbs. and in two weeks' time, I would be up 20 lbs. with noticeable muscle. That used to blow the counselors mind. I seemed to display the same pattern in the Army. I would lose rank on a regular basis for getting in trouble but would get it back almost as quick as I lost it. All I can ascertain from those patterns was a built in drive and determination, *below the deck.*

We lived on the 2700 block of Harlem Avenue in West Baltimore. As destiny would have it, a family moved directly across the street from our house that came from East Baltimore. One of the members in the family was a guy by the name of Clyde Wright. He lived in the basement of the house as well. A lot of guys in the area at that time that lived at home with their parents took the basement. He had the window of the basement open for air like most us did. Looking into his basement window, you could see these big weights up on a rack and a lifting platform underneath them. I have never seen a setup in someone's home quite like this before. This guy was a competitive power lifter and invited me over to workout with him. I made the decision to join him knowing that I wasn't in his league. I needed something else desperately to distract me from the usual destructive lifestyle that I had become accustomed to. Something that would uplift my self-esteem allowing me to make better decisions for myself, unlike I have ever experienced before. I believed this is it!

Going in the front door of his house, you would pass through the living room and the dining room and what was displayed all over the house were about 150 or so beautiful powerlifting trophies, won from different cities throughout the country. The majority of them were first-place trophies. Time would reveal that my buddy Clyde was qualified as one of the top five powerlifting champions in the country in his weight class. He was going to represent the US in the 1980 Olympics but could not go only because the US boycotted the Olympics that year. It was naturally a big disappointment for him but it didn't seem to dampen his spirit. From what I could tell, this guy seemed to eat, breathe, and live for powerlifting. He was squatting 600 pounds at a body weight of only 148 pounds. He was all-natural. Not one bad habit or vice that you could see.

YOUR DECISIONS DETERMINE YOUR DESTINY

Anyway, in the beginning of my connection to this brother, he put about 175 pounds on my back one day to squat and I was unable to do it. I was game but my body just wasn't up to it at the time. Still smoking weed on a regular basis and just dipping and dabbing a little with the hard stuff. Eight months later and still weighing 148 pounds, faithfully showing up he had me squatting 400 pounds in my first powerlifting competition. I won 3rd place in my division and I was happy as a peacock. I knew beyond the shadow of a doubt that this was the thing I'd been looking for, but just didn't know it. The next couple of years, I competed a few more times and picked up some nice trophies. That Hercules and Samson image of how I thought a man is supposed to look, (that I buried in the back of my mind as a kid) was coming to realization for me. I was fortunate enough to have one of the best teachers around.

He and I, and a couple more guys actually formed a weightlifting team with t-shirts that was named the *Daybreak Barbell Club*. On the back were words declaring, "*Setting records is our Business.*" Of course, not I at the time, but later years would reveal that I had it in me also. It appeared that I was leaning more towards pumping iron as opposed to pumping dope. I suppose almost any issue left unaddressed will eventually rear its ugly head in due time.

Couple years later my buddy Clyde had two studio audience tickets for a local TV show called *People are Talking*. This was around 1983. The two hosts that hosted the show was a guy name Richard Sher and Oprah Winfrey. On this particular live show, they had Arnold Schwarzenegger as a guest, showing the studio audience some basic stretching exercises. There was no sitting down the entire taping of this particular show. Arnold was finished with his bodybuilding career and was now mostly focused on movie roles. I shook his hand when I met him and realized that he is a pretty tall guy. A whole lot of women showed up for that show and the studio really couldn't accommodate the actual number of people that came. So what they did was made two groups with the smaller group consisting of only 9 people. Obviously, it made more sense to focus the TV camera on the small group of nine people that I was one of.

I Just Didn't Know

Let me try to depict the situation. Arnold was in front leading the exercises primarily facing the small group. It was three ladies in front, three ladies behind them, and three guys behind them, I was in the middle of the three guys at the rear of the group. Two factors that day: 1. Remember that the studio was very crowded because Arnold was there. 2. All the ladies decided to wear these very sexy, tight spandex types of outfits, including Oprah because once again, Arnold was there. When I say it was crowded in there, it was so tight that the small group of nine that I was in seemed to be right on top of each other. True but funny story: When Arnold directed us to bend over and touch our toes and hold it, I'll never forget this as long as I live. I bent over and touched my toes, no problem. When I lifted my head up and all I could see was six beautiful asses' inches from my face, in different rainbow colors. If I didn't say it, I'm sure I thought, "Good God Almighty." At 30 years old, I froze in my tracks for a minute while the rest of the eight participants continued movement led by Arnold's instructions. I believe I was too thrilled to be embarrassed.

My mother and my girlfriend were watching the show at home. When I got home, they asked me, why did I freeze on live TV? My answer was honest; "I was kind of caught off guard." I knew they were in front of me, but for that split second, I was a bit overwhelmed. I was a little flustered if anything, but I'm sure it could have happened to any 30-year-old young fella. At the end of the show, my buddy Clyde and I were standing out in the lobby of the TV studio before we left. Clyde was recently profiled in the number one powerlifting magazine entitled *Powerlifting USA*. He had Arnold autograph one of his profile article photos in the magazine of him dead lifting 600 lbs. at a body weight of 148 lbs. Incredible. I thought that was super cool and especially for me to witness it.

Now who was it that walked right by me, and lightly squeezed my right bicep and playfully said, "Ooh, look at those muscles?" None other than Miss Oprah Winfrey. At this time in her career, she was not that attractive to me and nowhere near as rich. I really didn't give it much thought except that gesture did put a little smile on my face. As I tell this story over the years I always say, had I known she would turn out to be the richest woman in the world, there would have not been any *Stedman*, trust me. Perhaps another missed opportunity?

CHAPTER 15
A Different Type of Wilderness

I managed to compete in the sport of powerlifting a few more times and picked up three additional trophies. As I continued training, I noticed that the need for *weed* was diminishing and my desire to shoot up heroin was on the increase. I knew I was a pot head from the word go, but it just seemed to stop working for me. Over the many years of smoking marijuana, my body had obviously developed a tolerance for this particular substance and demanded something much stronger. I recall going to a gym that one of my teammates from the Daybreak Barbell Club had started and attempted to train with weights. What was making it difficult for me was that I shot up some heroin not that long before I went to the gym. It sure didn't have the same affect that the weed had on me when I lifted. An internal spiritual warfare had taken place. My Aunt Pecolia described it as, "The flesh fighting against the spirit." I had actually fallen in love with the great sport of powerlifting. Yet, the strong pull and lure to do heroin was not only challenging this positive aspect of my life, but also threatening to override this new identity I had found. I had to make a decision. Either stop pumping iron or stop pumping dope in my arms.

Sadly, with a fast growing and progressive dope habit, the weightlifting lost out. Hopelessness had set in and the will to turn things back around was lost and broken. What had been very uplifting and inspiring to me, just wasn't important to me anymore. How can a young person such as myself allow such a downward spiral to take place? It's rightly classified as the *Disease of Addiction*. I began finding myself wondering around from place to place, staying wherever I haven't burned a bridge yet. I stayed with my brother Poochie and his wife for a short period of time, and although his wife Frances was an Angel of a woman, I was eventually uninvited. After a period of time I'm sure they had to reconcile with their decision. "Are we helping him or are we contributing to his dysfunction?" I just couldn't seem to get the normality of being responsible and consistently productive in society.

Let me make this point very clear, I'm not playing the blame game because my father was an alcoholic, because for nearly three years straight I got high in the Army by my own decision to do so. My brother Poochie got it right when he came back from Vietnam and began a career path towards being reliably stable. Not I. My brother and I would take a couple of trips to New York by way of Patterson, New Jersey where my older brother Gene lived. We would go *cop* some of that New York dope because it was cheaper and a better deal. Yes, my brother was caught up a little but not by any shape, form, or fashion like me, thank God. I never knew other people that *used* and didn't simultaneously destroy their life in the process. I was to be the so-called *black sheep* of the family, even though I don't agree with the word black always being portrayed in a negative sense, but I think you get the picture.

As my addiction grew, wherever I stayed at from this point, I stole whatever I could. I stole from my mother, father, sister, my nieces, my neighbors, my car washing clients, my uncles, and my 93 year old grandmother who was the only one left that would take me in, until I burned that bridge. If I could have stolen the morning dew and sold it to

A Different Type of Wilderness

get high, I would have. You have to understand that when you are caught up in the grip of addiction, everything goes and everybody goes. You are not living a life as most people are doing but surviving, existing as a mere shell of a human. You are no longer in a rational state of mind to make any kind of sound decisions; that is until you receive the *gift* of desperation. If the weather was too cold for me to do my reconditioning to cars, then I might go into a VA rehab just for a break in a desperate attempt to experience a little sanity. Two of my uncles, Uncle JP and Uncle Chump owned and operated a nightclub and combined liquor store. My uncle Chump asked me to start work for him selling booze on the cash register. That was a bad decision by him and a bad decision by me to do it at that time in my life. I'm not too certain what his mindset was but I'm sure he wanted to give me an opportunity to pull myself up at the same time, keeping the business in the family.

My addiction had really began to take off. In the neighborhood the nightclub was in, there were a lot of drugs. Before I even started my shift, I would go in the store with two bags of dope already in me, or in my pocket soon to go in me. I played that Dr. Jekyll and Mr. Hyde roll real good for a while. I was stealing money on a regular basis and eventually began to steal *top shelf* liquors. The real good stuff. Around six or seven months later, my uncle called me into his office downstairs and said, "Look, I got to let you go. Every time you work I never make any money." Actually, I was kind of glad he fired me, because I was so caught up, I just couldn't stop. It was a bit of a relief for me to stop hurting someone I looked up to and admired very much. However, when I left there, I had a serious heroin and morphine addiction; I suffered withdrawal pains from that level of addiction like you wouldn't believe. Just to walk one block would feel like someone beat me with a baseball bat before I was able to get that *fix*. I took myself into a living hell.

So I'm on the streets again back into the wilderness. I began sleeping wherever I could. I slept in abandoned buildings, in garages, the porches, in the bus station, in an abandoned car. Yes, I was officially homeless and when you're surviving in that type of lifestyle, it actually takes a lot of work. My downward spiral seemed to be picking up speed and you know what? I really didn't care at that point. As time went

YOUR DECISIONS DETERMINE YOUR DESTINY

on, I seemed to be connected to a subculture within society, detached from regular society. I would walk around sometimes as if I was a cast member of the *Walking Dead*. My weight was about 135 pounds soaking wet with rocks in my pocket.

I was surviving below animal level because at least animals do eat some type of food. I made a decision *not* to eat ongoing for four reasons: (1) Food would interfere with my high and it took too much work for me to *get on*; (2) the money spent on food would be a waste; and (3) Being that I was homeless, if I ate a meal, I might not keep it down, and (4) I was also faced with the dilemma of where could I go to do number two? I got tired of *pooping* in some secluded area on newspaper in a brown paper bag and then scraping my butt with newspaper or a brown paper bag. That did not feel good. It became my norm and part of the degradation I put myself through on a regular basis. I'm not sure if a real life Viking's ass could have put up with that. This was the life I was existing in. (Could it be the drugs?)

During this time, my father passed away. Even though I was a drug addict bum, I did view the body with my family at the funeral home. The next day, I reluctantly managed to stop by the house where a lot of people came by to give their condolences. My reluctance was due to the shameful and embarrassing way I was looking and I'm certain the unpleasant way I was smelling. God knows that I really wanted to be there to mourn and grieve my father's passing with the rest of my family, however, the way I was living and having my spirit inside completely bankrupt, I was too ashamed and embarrassed. I did manage to put my shame to the side for a moment and (it was very difficult), since I was, looking and smelling like a first-class bum. I recall at this sad time sitting at the dining room table reading one of the sympathy cards that was given with a $10 bill included. That's what a bag of dope cost, $10. That's all I thought about and what I truly lived for, a bag of dope. We're talking about a one-tracked selfish mind focused exclusively on one thing, drugs. I attempted to slide the 10 under the table with no one looking, so I thought. And then my eagle eye sister Vonnie who justifiably had me under surveillance, caught me and said with a low stern voice, "Put it back," and I complied to my surprise because I'm telling you, I was at a point in my life that I

A Different Type of Wilderness

didn't care for absolutely anyone, especially myself. I guess because of the somber atmosphere in the house, that I reluctantly gave in.

Although I did manage to view his body the day before, but the day of the funeral when my family was waiting for the limousine to pick them up, I'm sure the usual question arose, "Where is Stevie?" I must shamefully report that I was out committing burglaries to include my mother's home while my family went to bury my one and only father. I had to feed my dope habit. I was dope sick. I am thoroughly convinced that if he would have offered, I would have literally sold my soul to the devil for one bag of dope, without hesitation. Perhaps I already did, many times over without realizing it. At the time, I really believed that there was no hope for me and that I would eventually die with a needle in my arm or get killed for doing something stupid. The only thing that meant anything in the world to me was a bag of dope. My spirit was empty and completely vanquished. It was like when you blow a candle out, wasn't nothing left but a fading vapor. I was a mere shell of a man in every sense. I think you get the picture. One of the crazy things about it all was the fact that I was not alone out there, existing in the same manner. Later, in one of those drug Rehab's that I had went to when I was momentarily clean, I found myself grieving Daddy Carroll's passing by crying uncontrollably. The feeling just showed up one day it seemed out of nowhere since I didn't have any drugs in my body for that brief, short time. Obviously, that's exactly what I needed to experience since the narcotics previously denied me that opportunity.

So back on the streets roaming around with my mind on one thing and one thing only, I couldn't be trusted at all. You had to keep your eyes on me all the time because I will get you. After a while, Dr. Jekyll (the little front I was putting up) died, and Mr. Hyde took completely over. Needless to say, I still wasn't eating too much, which accounted for those 135 pounds I was carrying. At times, I would treat myself to 4/$1.00 doughnuts at *711* stores just to put *something* in me but not throw off the delicate balance of total dereliction, as I just recently described. Now to come up with that brilliant decision why I shouldn't eat food as long as I had my drugs in me for the reasons I previously described, clearly illustrates how completely detached I was from a normal way of living.

YOUR DECISIONS DETERMINE YOUR DESTINY

One night I was up on Belmont and Bloomingdale in West Baltimore, and the police pulled up on me real fast and asked me to come to the car. I had drugs and a syringe in my pocket. I'm still not too sure, how I pulled this off, but as I was approaching the patrol car, he had to take his eyes off me for a split second as he exited the car. In a fraction of a second, I pulled the needle and the drugs swiftly from my pocket and slipped them under his patrol car. When he searched me, I was clean. Told me to step off and I did and then waited for them to pull off. When they did, I immediately retrieved what was mine. While I'm on the streets, you tend to keep a sharp eye out and in my old neighborhood, I discovered that this lady, who happened to be a good friend of my mother's, decided to go on vacation. I then decided to sneak in the upstairs back balcony window to gain entrance. I stayed there as if I lived there. Didn't have much of an appetite and didn't find it necessary to wash up. When I slept in other places such as abandoned buildings, garages, etc., I use to wash my face by taking my index finger, wetting it with my tongue, and then wipe the crap from around my eyes as I'm making my way to go make it happen.

Anyway, I'm in this lady's house, naturally, I begin to take small things out to sell until I decided to go for the washing machine in the basement. It was almost brand-new. I'm facing a challenge; I don't want to invite anyone in on this *caper*. I am a smart guy when I want to be (according to me). First, I go find a potential customer for the merchandise. Once that was established, I went down into the basement and opened the basement outside door, which had about four or five steps down to it. I can't scratch it because then the price would go down. I get two flat pieces of long wood measuring the length of the steps, a rope, and a blanket. By myself at a weight of 135 pounds, I pulled that heavy wash machine out of that basement and set it in the backyard. Real motivation will give you the capacity to do almost anything. Once I removed it from the basement's holding grip, *then* I got someone to help me carry it to the destination.

When that lady of the house returned home, she was furious. I heard that she began to gather her own intelligence on this crime by simply asking the neighbors did they see anyone carrying a washing machine through the alley. Somebody fingered me. She sent the police to the

A Different Type of Wilderness

guy's house I sold it to and got her property back. Of course, I was long gone and I didn't have a chance to make amends at least to the recipient until some 15 years later. Fortunately, she didn't press charges once she regained her property back and I strongly believe that was because she was friends with my mother.

CHAPTER 16

Joining Up With Danger

So I'm still on the streets, cleaning cars where ever I can. Lying, stealing, and doing whatever is necessary to get my hands on some money. My drug habit is still picking up momentum and it appears that getting high is the driving force of my life. Although I have faint hopes of a better life, I just can't embrace the reality of a *normal* life. During this time, I met my oldest daughter Morgan's mother. I was shampooing the inside of this vehicle in an alley way that is adjacent to the elementary school #202 and she came walking by. I said to myself, "Wow, look at that pretty chocolate woman." I evidently caught her eye as well. I realized that I had virtually nothing to offer anyone except a shell of a man. We hooked up and immediately began using together. She was on the methadone program, and I was on my heroin addiction. An attraction made for hell, to say the least.

On Fridays, I would travel downtown to University Hospital where she received her methadone. University dispensed a certain high quality

YOUR DECISIONS DETERMINE YOUR DESTINY

brand of methadone widely known as the *biscuit*. Friday is when she received her dose for the day and an additional two bottles called *take homes* for the weekend. They never made it home. Just around the corner from the methadone clinic is the world famous *Lexington Market*. To the underworld, it is also a well know place for people that were not on the meth program seeking to purchase people's take home bottles. Every weekend faithfully, we would sell her two bottles for 80 bucks apiece. We would then travel back uptown to purchase me either a bag of morphine or a bag of heroin. Simultaneously, she would buy some cocaine to collaborate with the meth that she has in her already. That combination used to baffle me and I really did not see the point of it, until I got myself on a short-term methadone program and then I could see the point of it. It's just this simple, methadone is a strong downer to replace heroin and hold you for quite some time with no relief in sight. Cocaine on the other hand is an upper and it sort of counteracts the strong down feeling and kind of levels you off. Before you try to make any sense out of it, remember that using drugs is an expression of insanity. We wind up sharing two different apartments and losing two different apartments as a result of our drug use. While having our beautiful daughter Morgan, in the process.

Before Morgan was born, we were evicted out of our first apartment together located on the corner of Arlington and Mosher Streets in West Baltimore. Leslie was collecting a welfare check and the mailman handed her check over to her even though we no longer resided there. He told us very clearly and stern that next month he would not give us the check at this address. In other words, we need to give the welfare office a new address. A month later, we had no new address and were waiting on the stoop for the mailman to come on check day. The same mailman shows up and said, "Didn't I tell you that you need a new address to receive this check?"

We said, "Yeah, but shit happens."

His response was, "Well I'm not giving it to you." This was a rather big size brother I would say around 200lbs and perhaps 6ft tall. Of course, I'm still packing about 135lbs, soaking wet.

Joining Up With Danger

So we proceeded in following this federal employee as he was delivering mail and I started threatening him saying, "Oh, you are going to give us that check." I then reached down to the ground and picked up this nice size rock that filled my out stretched hand and simply said, "If you don't give me that check I'm going to bust your head open." I'm sure I made that threat with conviction. As this brother was moving along he looked back and seen me almost on his heels.

He then at that point surrendered and said, "Don't you think that I'm afraid of you, here, take it and get away from me." We then went and did what we always did; shoot up drugs. I sometimes wondered what I would have done if he didn't release that check? I do know that sheer desperation is a terrible thing.

One evening Leslie and I were lying in bed and just got finished having sex. She said I need to tell you something about me. She shared a secret with me that would come in handy a little later down the road. She told me about two or three years before we met, she and a guy pulled a liquor store robbery. The man behind the counter reached for a gun and she blasted him. She caught a homicide charge as a result. She wound up doing no more than three years down in Jessup State Prison because of the overcrowded prison population. I asked her was it necessary for you to kill him? She said, "Honestly, it was either me or him."

I replied with I'm thinking some comforting assurance. "You had to do what you had to do"

As a result of cleaning cars in the professional fashion that I did, one of my customers who happened to be a wholesale cocaine drug dealer, referred me to an associate of his, a guy by the name of *T* that had an auto repair garage. I didn't get it at first that *T* stood for trouble, but I would later. While cleaning this guy's car one day, he offered me a proposition to work exclusively for him, promising to pay me very well. With not too many good options on the table, I made a decision to go that way. Come to find out that the garage was a mere front for his successful cocaine business. I realized it and it became very evident when he came into the garage one day, dumped a big pile of cash on the table, and began to

YOUR DECISIONS DETERMINE YOUR DESTINY

count it. My first response was a sarcastic question of, "Are you a banker or something?" Did that turn me away? No, it turned me on. In other words, he said forget about cleaning cars and exclusively focus on drug dealing. Not a smart decision but how can you make a good decision living by desperation.

He used to stash his ounces of what they called *fish scale raw cocaine* way up in the ceiling of the garage. He used a very tall ladder to stash it. Then he tells me, "Let's forget about those cars because I need you to be my lieutenant for my operations."

"Cool," I replied. He had multiple selling houses and would sometimes position me in them armed with this brand-new AK-47 on ready for the stickup boys. I didn't actually sell the product myself, just performed guard duty, and watched the count. He told me about an incident of this guy sticking up one of his houses, but was unable to catch him. One day the police knocked on the door of one of the houses I was in. I kind of panicked and flushed the entire product, which was considerable, down the toilet. When T came by and I told him what happened, he acted as if he didn't believe me. So he proceeded to flush some himself down the toilet to see if they would go. Some of the tightly packed small plastic vials did flush down, and some floated. I maintained my claim, and he just had to get over it. He was paying me somewhat of a decent pay, however, I believe he could have been paying more for the risk I was taking.

For a while, I was staying in the basement of Leslie's mother's house right behind Carver High School, without her mom's knowledge. I was sneaking in and sneaking out but of course, I had plenty of drugs with me. As stated earlier, she and I had lost the two different apartments as a result of us being irresponsible and putting getting high over and above everything else. T had dropped me off or picked me up from my mother's house once or twice although I wasn't living there.

I eventually decided to rent a room from my buddy Tommy down on Gilmore Street, where he and his girlfriend lived. I grew up on Harlem Avenue with this guy. It was just a room with a little kitchen in it, not that

Joining Up With Danger

I was cooking anything, and I had a little small black and white TV set in there. Oh yeah, I seen a couple of huge ass rats not running, but actually galloping in the back of the kitchen area. Never quite seen anything like that before.

Anyway, I'm sitting up in the room one Sunday afternoon watching a little TV and I get a knock on the door. I opened the door and it was my man T and this other guy. Once inside the room, my man T pulls out a gun and says, "This is the guy I was telling you about that stuck up my houses," and my first thought was, why in the hell did you bring him here? This guy was a known stickup man, a true street soldier. And this guy had evidently heard that when T catches up which you, he will put a couple of hot slugs up in you.

So as the guy was going by the window pulling the curtain back, I assume he was looking for a way out and at the same time saying, "Naw man it wasn't me you got the wrong guy."

Next thing I knew, he reached for the gun in T's hand, and they hit the floor scuffling for possession of that gun while it was going off. It's starting to get real crazy up in here. One minute I'm sitting in the room watching TV and the next minute I'm ducking and dodging bullets coming out of that barrel. Then I hear my man T says, "Steve, get the gun." I'm thinking now hold up a minute. Last thing I knew you had the gun and now you are going to let this frightened for his life, man, take this gun, and shoot you and me. Everything was happening so fast. Afraid for my life, I grabbed a short pipe that was lying in the room (don't know where it came from) and began beating this guy in the head hoping that would weaken him. This guy was afraid for his life and very desperate. I continued whacking him in the head with that pipe until his head started spurting blood like a water fountain.

Then I heard T say, "I got it," which gave me a big relief. The guy got up blood running down his face, threatened to get T and myself, first chance he can. Didn't realize until a little later that during that scuffling on the floor, the guy caught a slug in his back. This was a tough boy. He still got up and ran up out of there.

YOUR DECISIONS DETERMINE YOUR DESTINY

    This block of Gilmore Street was right around the corner from the Mount Street police station. In fact, the next block over. As a result of the gunshots being fired, someone probably called the police. Now the guy left first, two minutes later T slides me the bloody gun and says do something with this, and he left. Blood was on me and everywhere so I went up to the second floor where the bathroom was and proceeded to wash the blood off my hands and arms. Took my bloody t-shirt off and threw it in the corner. My buddy Tommy, who I was renting the room from, was listening with his girlfriend, to what was going on downstairs. He commented to me, "Y'all were trying to kill that guy."

    Before I could respond to him, there was a knock on the door stating "Police." Seconds later, they knocked harder stating louder, "Police." Next thing, *boom*, they are in the building. This was actually a three-story building. So I made it to the third floor and on to the roof while they searched the house. I had to crouch and hide on the roof because *foxtrot*, the police helicopter was on the scene. Right next door to the building we were in was this church and they were having some type of evening service.

    Once the coast was clear, I slid down off of their roof down to this fence that separated the two yards. I jumped to the fence, and then to the ground and kind of twisted my ankle a little. I thought about Leslie's mother's house which wasn't too far away, so with no shirt on, blood on my sneakers, I jogged a few blocks away jabbing and punching in the air as if I was exercising or training. Made it to her mom's house, went down to the basement and my ankle swelled up so much that I demanded her to call an ambulance, and she did. There goes the secret of me sneaking down there even though I had that room. Later I found out that the guy I beat with that pipe was in the hospital for a week with his head swelled up. A week later, Tommy told me that him and his brother returned and busted in that room like *John Shaft* looking for me, but I was long gone. This guy, understandably so, wanted me real bad. When I hooked back up with my man T, I told him that he owes me *big time*.

CHAPTER 17
A Decision for Suicide

Living this type of lifestyle if you can call it that, as insane as it was, required work and thoughtful concentration. I'm still working for this guy named T, but I'm still homeless and laying my head down almost anywhere, I can. Oftentimes when I slept in someone's garage, I would come to in the morning, and as I did before, wash my face by wetting my index finger with my tongue and then proceed to wipe the sleep out of my eyes. I would find a scrub brush in a bucket, and attempt to brush my hair. I would then take off.

I'm lying up in this garage one night and I'm thinking, T owes me some money and he has not been treating me fair. I am really feeling so disgusted and frustrated with myself that I'm open to almost any kind of lame brain idea. I know what would fix me! So at that point, I decided to stick T up, rob him with his own weapon. One of the worst decisions I ever made in my life. I had a plan. I let him drop me off at his garage.

YOUR DECISIONS DETERMINE YOUR DESTINY

When he left, I went high up in the ceiling and took several ounces of his raw cocaine. I then went and grabbed his brand-new AK-47 and placed it in position where I could easily reach it, upon his return. I was afraid, anxious, and desperate at this point. I didn't even allow myself to think this decision through. What would be the consequences if I got away with the stick-up? Actually, once I decided to go through with it, I really didn't care about the imminent consequences. I just couldn't continue on existing day to day, as I was.

When he returned and walked through the big garage door, which was propped up by a tall piece of wood, I placed myself in position and kicked out the wood. The large garage door came down fast and hard, (boom). I got his attention real quick. I then produced the AK-47, ordered him over to the desk, and told him to put all of his cash on the desktop, along with all of his jewelry. I told him that he wasn't treating me right, so I have to take what I believe he owes me, and extra. Keep in mind this guy has already shot up a couple of guys for robbing him, that's why the guy he brought to my room that day was afraid for his life. Added the fact that I was not a tough guy whatsoever, but I was desperate and desperation exceeds all boundaries. He seemed shocked that I was actually pulling this off, and guess what? So was I. I then told him to put his car keys on the desktop while I have this loaded and aimed AK-47 pointed at him, which I knew he respected a great deal.

Now for my getaway. I took all of the ounces of raw fish scale cocaine, perhaps 9 or 10 ounces valued at a considerable amount of money, perhaps at least 40 to 50K on the streets (depending how you package it up), all the cash that he had available, his gold jewelry, and his car keys. As I was leaving out the door, I put a little chain on the outside of the door and told him if I see the door move before I'm gone, I am going to come back in and kill him. I got in his Audi and started it up, and seen the chain on the door rattling as he was trying to free himself. I then pulled up right to the door and said, "I see that I have to come in and kill you."

He replied through the door saying, "Naw man, just go ahead I'm cool," and then left the door alone, thank God. I don't believe I had it in me under normal circumstances; however, this was far from normal. I

A Decision for Suicide

was so glad that he didn't persist in calling my bluff. I then took off and headed uptown thinking about my next move. As I was driving down Park Heights Avenue I seen a cab driving beside me and I beckoned him to pull over and he did. I then pulled behind the Taxi Cab and parked. I was able to stash the money, and it was a lot, jewelry, and most of the ounces of cocaine on my person, almost as I did walking into that Social Security building I used to work in. I left the AK-47 in the car and a couple of ounces and told the cab driver that my car was acting up and had him drop me off in my neighborhood, another deadly decision. I soon returned to the car that same evening, picked up that assault rifle, the rest of the drugs and thought that I was *the man*. *I was* the man, *a marked man!*

As I said, I foolishly returned to the hood where I was known. Imagine being broke all the time, homeless, not eating, or washing myself as my norm, and then instantly transformed into a man with plenty of money, plenty of drugs and the respect that goes with it. When you have a lot of drugs and plenty of money, everybody wants to invite you in, but also sell you out just as fast. So I'm trying not to be visible on the streets because I know this guy wants me with a deep passion. So I'm cautiously moving about making money and on the run. What convinced me that I can sell *his* drugs in *my* neighborhood and live eludes me to this day. I knew people that had been killed for doing the exact same thing.

I watched him closely as he showed me how to make fast money. What you do is make the *weight* of your product ridiculously heavier than the competition and always keep it pure. With that methodology, I was making $1000 in one hour and then I would move somewhere else quickly. I heard that my man T had stopped by my mother's house looking for me. She had never met him before and he coldly told her to her face that when he sees me, he will kill me. I can't imagine the terror and the horror that my dear my mother felt from hearing that from a total stranger. Momma wasn't in great health to begin with and that added stress had to contribute to her declining health. When he left her house, he left a car parked on the block waiting for me to show up. Meanwhile, I'm insanely moving around with this money, drugs, and the assault rifle tucked in a wrap.

YOUR DECISIONS DETERMINE YOUR DESTINY

Eventually I began to see faces that I've never seen before with a distinct look of *I think you're the one*. I'll never forget that look for as long as I shall live. I needed a good hideout. I went up in my buddy David's apartment who lived overtop of this Korean corner store in the 600 block of Ashburton Street. You had to enter around back up these metal stairs over top of the store and there was only one door, and one window beside that one door at the back of the apartment. It was two windows at the front but they were directly over the top of the store. I got the word on the street that I had a contract on my head. My uncle that owned that nightclub that I used to work at and steal from used his people to find out that it was for $15,000. It sounds like a lot, but I have witnessed him making that in less than a week's time. I have seen people get whacked for $100 or less.

Any rate, back up in David's apartment while we were getting high, (always plenty of freeloaders available) and then we hear someone playing with that one and only door. I didn't mind the freeloaders that much because I looked at it as a *blurred crowd* around me. Now I was already paranoid and for good reason. I began to get extremely fearful and against David's wishes, I proceeded to take a hammer and some nails and nail the one and only door shut. David then responded by saying, "Man, what in the hell is wrong with you?"

I then replied, "Look man, its people out there that are trying to kill me, or capture me and take me back to a guy who is waiting to kill me himself. This shit is real. Besides, you didn't have a problem with me coming in here sharing free drugs with you, did you? So, just be quiet and be cool and hope this don't turn out too bad."

He had a skylight on the roof and the hired assassins began to try and pry the skylight cover loose from the outside, to gain entry into the apartment. I then began to start shooting some rounds through the skylight and they backed off. Everyone in the apartment that was freely getting high started freaking out. Truth is, no one wants to get hit with an AK 47 slug. I believe they fell back all the way and focused on regrouping. Some time went by and when the coast was clear, I slipped out of one of the front windows overtop of the store, hung and dropped to the ground

A Decision for Suicide

and ran up the alley and hid out in this guy's basement in the 2800 block of Harlem Avenue.

I was going to try to hide out in another buddy's house right up the alley way by the name of James Hayes. When I went through the alley and stood at his fence to his backyard, his window was open. I kept hearing him repeat over and over again inside of his house, what obviously someone drilled him with was, "Where is he at? Where is he at? Where is he at?" over and over again in a real frantic voice. Almost like, he was traumatized by those hit boys.

I told myself after hearing that, "I'm not going in there." Hell, he was scaring me more. I kept it moving.

I needed to go buy some bags for my product and I needed someone I thought I could trust. Someone that would watch my back and take care of business when needed. So I got in touch with Leslie, although pregnant at the time with my oldest daughter. I put a .38 caliber I picked up along the way in her hand and positioned her to cover my back. I remembered not too long after she and I first got together, when she shared that secret with me. So she was qualified to watch my back with commitment. However, her being also a committed drug addict like myself, she would eventually steal from me when I didn't give her everything she wanted. It's all in the game and it's not personal.

One night I surfaced and was on the street for a little while. I knew I was being hunted and my family begged me to leave town. Greed overruled common sense. I was making too much money, even though I had a price on my head. That night I came out for some stupid reason without any weapons on me. I seen a couple guys that was on T's payroll and they gave me chase. I saw a couple more guys that were out for me. I think because I kept getting away up to this point, he went all out, and had the entire perimeter covered with guys in place unknowingly to me. I even ran under the Edmondson Avenue Bridge in the park and there were a couple of guys there. I couldn't believe it. Literally, guys were everywhere. I'm actually living out a nightmare I think I seen in a movie before. But this is death defying reality. I'm scared out of my wits,

YOUR DECISIONS DETERMINE YOUR DESTINY

but I can't stop and I must keep moving. The first law of nature: Self Preservation is very real when put to the *do or die* test.

This is the picture, no matter what direction I ran, there would be dudes in place, some on foot and some in cars. They were all united in one accord, to get me! I had eventually sold the AK 47, a premature decision that paralleled my decline. I ran and I ran and I ran. I felt like the loneliest person on earth that night. I couldn't process or realize any kind of *big picture* behind this decision, But I was so grateful for the instinct to keep living. They chased me up in this alley in the 2000 block of Arunnah Avenue and as I hit the alley, up on the other end were guys up there, waiting. I figure at least 15 to 20 guys were out covering that perimeter, waiting for me to surface. As I ran about in the middle of the alley, I randomly ran up on this back porch and feverishly knocked on the door. This was about 1:30 AM. As they were approaching from both ends of the alley, I'm getting frantic and in deep panic mode. A lady came to the door looking through the glass asking me what I want. I stated, "I need to use your phone and I have an emergency on my hand."

She then stated, "Mr., will you please get off my porch." Of course, I'm looking left to right and they are approaching closer. It seemed like their coordinated approach from both ends of the alley were methodical and cautious. As a matter of fact, the porch was about 10 to 12 stairs high and I was almost certain I heard someone under the porch. At that point, she had a big wide triple pane glass kitchen window. Something told me, "Go through it." I did. I crashed through all of that glass and the only cut's I incurred was a cut on the top of my left hand and a small cut on my elbow. I didn't have time to think or feel. The adrenaline was coursing through my body so strong that all I could run on was instinct. I proceeded through the kitchen, through the dining room, and then through the living room and out the front door. I knew that I had to keep it moving. The woman whose house I just randomly invaded was standing on her next-door neighbor's porch with a meat cleaver in her hand. Simultaneously the police pulled up, she obviously and wisely had urgently called them.

I walked down the steps off the porch and leaned on the hood of the police car and it took me about 5 to 10 minutes to catch my breath.

A Decision for Suicide

Because those hit boys ran me like crazy. God was with me. After I caught my breath and putting blood on the hood of the car, the cops asked what happened. I told them that I was going to the Chinese joint to get some food and as I was counting my money, these guys seen me and began chasing me. Don't know if they fully brought that story, that's what I gave them. Naturally, the woman of the house that I just crashed through sharing my night of terror with wanted her window replaced. I asked her how much would it cost. She said around perhaps $160. I had $80 in my pocket and told her I would bring her the rest tomorrow when I get off work. (As if, I had a real job). She went with it.

The cops asked me did I need a ride. Hell yeah, I told them. As they were taking me to another house that I had drugs stashed down at the 2100 block of Edmondson Avenue, I was looking out of the back window to see if we were being tailed. Didn't see anyone following us, but they were. Anyway, they dropped me off at this girl's house and the freeloaders there started to freak out when they observed me pulling up in this police car. Naturally, they didn't know what to think. I go in and relieve their concerns and fears, go upstairs where they were getting high and told them what just happened.

Something told me to go back downstairs and check. As I was walking down the steps, I could see straight through the living room and I noticed a figure jumping back out of sight from one of the two tall front windows. Here we go again. I still had that .38 revolver stashed that I haven't sold yet as I continue to spiral downward. It was getting light outside by now and the girl's house I was at had a guy friend of hers parked outside across the street. She wouldn't let him in the house as long as the *candy man* (me), was there. When the coast was clear, I propositioned him to drive me to a place down on Carey Street right up from my uncle's club. I don't know how I got past that look out guy, but I did. Anyway, when I got down there, I snuck around back, went up the fire escape steps to the third floor, climbed in a window, and fell asleep on some people's bed that I knew, but they did know I was up there. Left with my calling card, blood on the sheet.

CHAPTER 18
Downhill Fast

Life for me by now just seems to be endless with the insanity I keep deciding to entertain. Came dangerously close to getting bumped off, yet still I keep choosing to not get out. It's almost as if life is on automatic pilot and I just don't seem to have the ability to change course, as much as I need to. I tried something different and I placed myself on a 21-day methadone detox program. Continuing to use heroin leaves me with absolutely no light at the end of the tunnel. My motives are not that clear with this move, it's as if I just came up with the idea. I have already sampled a good taste of it from one of Leslie's weekend take home bottles and realized how strong that stuff is. That small portion that I drank had me high for over two days straight. Truth of the matter was, I wasn't ready to get my act together. It turned out I got on the methadone to get off the heroin and then I got back on the heroin to get off the methadone. A bit of contradiction to say the least. A vicious unending cycle rendering me incapable of breaking free.

I met this one brother that was on the program and on the same day, we hooked up and went uptown to this other brother's house by the name

YOUR DECISIONS DETERMINE YOUR DESTINY

of Bruce. Always thinking of any kind of possibility. I had previously gone back to my uncle Jesse and borrowed his buffer machine to make some money. Jesse still trusted me a great deal at this time, especially for him to turn over his buffer to me. As my fate would have it, I eventually put the buffer in the pawn shop, with no legitimate intent on getting it out. In my right mind, I would have never disrespected Jesse in that way. Our relationship was special and we have gotten pretty close over the years working together. As I stated earlier, he never had any children and I think he kind of looked at me as a son rather than his nephew. Plus from his own prior personal experience, I knew that he could relate to being caught up. So what, I now start justifying the slimy things I'm doing because of that?

I later asked to borrow his small Isuzu pickup truck, before he realized that his buffer machine was in the pawn shop. He reluctantly let me have it and told me I better come back with his truck at a certain time. I took his truck, his only transportation at the time, and kept it over a week. It's easy to understand why and how an addict can abuse and misuse those (family) that are close to him. Because of the emotional connection, family is more vulnerable and susceptible to be victims. Now when myself and that guy that I met on the program went up to Bruce's house, I was driving and he had with them a real nice 9 mm gun. He decided to leave it out in the truck under the seat when we went in the house to get high. Always scheming and looking for a way to get over, I stated that I had forgotten something in the truck and went back out to the truck, jumped in and took off. I did a bunch of slimy things.

Of course, my man was pissed and I heard that he went back down to the methadone clinic where I met him; I'm sure with another gun looking for me. Needless to say, I never went back to the clinic. So I'm riding around with my uncle's unauthorized use of his truck, a 9 mm under the seat. I knew that my mother was worried about me to no end so I slipped by there one day when the coast was clear and went inside the back way to try to lessen her fears and worry.

There is no way that I could ever imagine the living nightmare that her youngest child, put her through. The terror and horror that was on

Downhill Fast

her face when she finally saw me, I'll never forget as long as I live. It was as if she was looking at a dead son on his way to the graveyard. From my viewpoint, it looked like mamma was on the verge of a nervous breakdown. I can't imagine the heavy burden that I put on her nerves, day after day, and night after night. I did feel real bad looking at her with my own eyes, the irrefutable pain, and suffering that I and I alone inflicted. I'm sure she was frantically waiting to hear the terrible news about her baby boy, getting killed. I truly thought I was easing her worry when I lifted up my shirt producing that big 9 mm to say I have protection mamma, I have a weapon on me out in these streets. Dumb decision. She almost had that nervous breakdown when she seen that gun. She gasped in a faint, dry voice, "Oh Jesus, Lord have mercy." She knew that the horrific drama I was living out was all too real. When I produced that big gun, she had to feel it down to her very soul. My mother was not accustomed to anything with the slightest of resemblance, of what I was putting her through. I remember her frantically saying, "Just go Stevie, go." She just couldn't take it. As I turned away and headed for the door, I heard mamma saying, "Lord Jesus, I'm going to bury my baby boy." When she said that, a cold chill sort of passed through my body.

Up to this point, my feelings and emotions were numb to almost everything. But I felt those words that she uttered through a trembling voice. Anyway, I slipped back out making sure the coast was clear to see what I might be able to pull off. I stopped back down on Gilmore Street, where I beat that man in the head, to see what was up. My Uncle Jesse obviously knew where to find me. He appeared out of nowhere in the middle of the street telling me quite insistently, to pull over. He was highly pissed at me, understandably so. Told me to get out of his truck and I did, apologizing and grabbing that 9 mm from under the seat. When he seen that gun, he just simply told me, "Boy, you going to jail." Obviously, an unavoidable destination.

As I continued to run the streets as a wanted man, things begin to take a turn faster than I could imagine. Yes, I was still making a little money, but I had a heroin habit and now a cocaine habit that was sucking the very life out of me. As the saying goes, a monkey can't sell bananas. At one point, I was making thousands of dollars in a few hours and before I knew

YOUR DECISIONS DETERMINE YOUR DESTINY

it, the decline took me to first selling the AK-47 for $500, and eventually selling a .38 caliber that I exchanged for drugs at next to nothing, then of course finally, the 9mm. The progression of the disease of addiction is quiet and invisible. How and why would one remain in an area where people are actually planted to kill you? A combination of insanity and desperation. Before I knew it, as fast as I rose up, I came down even faster. Remember, *a monkey can't sell bananas*.. I had no more drugs to sell and no more money pouch filled with cash.

I was a junkie on the streets of West Baltimore doing my best to survive and to stay alive. What I couldn't steal, rob, beg, or borrow; I did whatever I needed to do. Me and this other drug addict were on the streets together one day. He got lucky before I did and bought his self a much-needed bag of dope. At the blink of an eye when he took his eyes off me, I quickly put a knife to his throat and told him to hand it over. Even he could hardly believe I would stoop so low as to stick him up for a $10 bag of dope. It's as if I was going downhill 90 mph. It gets worse. I stood in front of the 7-Eleven convenient stores on several occasions *panhandling* (a nice polite word for begging) for change. I also went across the street to the gas stations begging for change. I then began to pull off some daytime burglaries. Another buddy of mine who wasn't as bad off as I was, easily convinced me to go inside people's homes and bring out appliances. We walked out big TV's together and other items that we could get some fast money for. This was a lonely, very cold existence.

I was actually detached from society, as we perceive it and became a starring cast member of a subculture group that resembled the *Night of the Living Dead*. I'm not eating unless I treat myself to four for a dollar doughnuts from 7-Eleven. That was my meal. Any and all other money must go for my drug habit. At this time, I'm on the run from the *hit boys* and from the police. I heard that a friend of mines mother's house would be unoccupied for a short period of time, just like before, I made a decision to move in. I made my entrance through the upstairs back balcony window, and that's where I went in and out. Just like before, as the days went by, I began to take various items from the house that I could quickly sell. One day I was in there, my friend's mother popped-up and returned. I was upstairs hiding but I just got finished smoking a

Downhill Fast

cigarette, probably one I found on the ground. She came upstairs and said, "Somebody has been smoking in here." She quickly left and before I had a chance to make my exit she went and got a hold of my buddy Kurt, the one that I had sold that washing machine to. He found me up in there, threatened me, and told me to get my ass up out of there, which I quickly obliged.

Now I'm back on the street ducking and dodging the eminent danger that awaits me. As I'm walking through one of the alleys, (which was the frequent route I had to take), I see a police car and I noticed that they were beaming on me. I began to run ducking to another alley and then realized there were more than one police car on the chase. I was becoming successful in shaking the cops loose as I navigated those alleys day by day, that I came to know so well. What I wasn't aware of at the time was that *Foxtrot*, the police helicopter was in on the chase. I went to a backyard and opened these two heavy metal doors that led down to the basement. It was about four maybe five steps under those two metal doors. They didn't seal completely when closed but left a crack between them. Next thing I knew, all inside of that little cubbyhole was lit up brighter than the noonday sun. *Foxtrot* had some powerful searchlights attached to it. They then communicated to the ground police cars my exact location. I come up out of there and tried to make a break for it but they had squad cars in every direction of the alley. Okay, they got me.

I recall the cops using their patrol cars unnecessarily to almost pin me with their front bumpers facing each other. I guess they call themselves having a little fun. It seemed like everybody was outside watching all of this commotion. As they were handcuffing me and putting me in the back of the patty wagon, another friend of mine's mother, Miss Florence, was on the scene and asked me, "Boy, what have you done?"

My reply was, "I haven't done anything."

And she was like, "Yeah okay." I strongly believe that before I made it down to the police station and got booked, my family was informed. Bad news always travels fast, as they say.

CHAPTER 19
Baltimore City Jail

I had previously spent the night a couple of different times in a jail precinct station, but this is the first time at the age of 35 years old when I'm going to actually be here for a while. Throughout the years as I was coming up, almost every guy I knew did some time in jail dating as far back as when I was in my teens. Should I as well, just like them, supposed to have done *time* for the many crimes I committed? Absolutely, without a doubt. I was apparently a late bloomer with doing time and having kids. As we left the jail precinct after being booked, they loaded us up on a bus headed for the city jail; I'm not quite sure what I was feeling. Whatever it was that awaited me, had to include a much-needed break from the madness I was living. I was originally booked for Illegal Entry and Burglary and my bail was set at $25,000. I didn't feel too bad about those charges because I'm thinking this is lightweight and I'll probably be released the first time they take me to court.

Entering the Baltimore City Jail (BCJ) system, although it's not a state prison, was a sober moment for me in more ways than one. All of the overcrowding that I had heard about was clearly evident. More and

YOUR DECISIONS DETERMINE YOUR DESTINY

more people (African Americans) were getting locked up to the point that they literally didn't know where to put them, but of course, they made room. I felt a bit uneasy in this new environment and soon realized that it was my decisions that landed me there. When I was received in the BCJ courtside, they searched the records a little deeper, as customary, and they charged me an Attempted Murder charge for beating that guy in the head with that pipe. I had unknowingly left a piece of paper with my name on it in that room I was renting, and that's how they charged me. At first, I thought my boy Tommy gave me up. Then I realized later that although there were shots fired that was reported, and a bloody mess everywhere, they didn't have the victim at that time until they obviously caught up with him in the hospital. The cops quickly put it together with the name they had for the crime.

That bail at first was set at $100,000, and then they decided to upgrade it to No Bail. I asked the cop what exactly does that mean. The cop pleasingly informed me with a smile on his face, "You're not going anywhere." I started off by going into C-section, one of the very large receiving parts of the jail. I had a dope habit coming into jail and weighing about 135 pounds. They put me in a two-man cell and on some occasions, they made it a three-man cell due to the overcrowding. A very tight situation and it was hot as hell in that cell. Second day there, I ran into a guy who was on my cellblock that I knew on the streets. I'm feeling worse as each new day begins from the withdrawal. Admittedly, while on the streets, I was shooting drugs in my system all day and every day. Now it's reckoning time! He told me, (the guy I knew from the streets), that the boy that I beat with that pipe was in our section, but he also told the boy that I was there too, like a double agent. I remember feeling even more uneasy and tense. How and when is this thing going to jump off? There is nowhere to run and hide when you are locked up.

I came out of my cell that morning headed to breakfast and before I made it to the entrance of this great big dining hall, the guy that I beat with that pipe had been there already for a couple of months and was working on the serving line. He hopped over the serving line and ran all the way through this huge dining hall running towards me saying, "I'm going to kill him." Before I knew it, we connected and hit the floor, now

Baltimore City Jail

I'm scared, and out of what must have been survival instinct; I had him on the floor locked down in a way that he couldn't move. I wasn't thinking at all, just reacting to this threat. I wasn't in any kind of physical shape compared to my adversary, however, I knew about desperation very well. I guess maybe some old muscle memory kicked in from underneath my drug-addicted body. It happened so fast just when I was about to give him a good shot, he tried to bite my jugular vein (remember we are in jail), and then the guards came and snatched us apart. As they were taking us both to L section (lock up), he was yelling to me all of these things he was going to do to me, one was, "You're going to be my bitch."

I yelled back, "Yeah mother#@&*, who was the bitch that was just on the floor and couldn't move unless I let you?"

As an amateur in the *joint,* my fear must have made me get with the program real quick. They put us in individual lockdown cells just for six days. When I got in my cell, I realized that when I had him on the floor, I must have twisted my back a little, my back was killing me. I will not lie; I was scared to death, especially after all those *wolf tickets* (inviting someone to fight you), that this cat was selling. I truly wasn't in any kind of (working out) shape and just coming from the streets with a serious dope habit. I repeat, I was really scared. After swelling this guy's head up with that pipe and having him lying up in the hospital for a week, he wanted me as bad as he wanted air to breathe. I knew he could just taste beating my ass up. I also knew that in six days I would have to face this guy either out in the yard or on the tier, since we were in the same cellblock section.

The second day on lockup, I started stretching a little, my back killing me while mostly focusing on the rematch that awaited me. I started painfully touching my toes and going side to side. Despite the physical pain I was in, and the apparent fear I was experiencing, it seemed like my competition training mentality kicked in. In other words, I have experienced training with sore and aching muscles. The third day I started stretching more and realized that I do have some muscle memory.

There was a young boy in the lock down cell next to me. Although we couldn't see each other, we began to talk a little. I shared with

YOUR DECISIONS DETERMINE YOUR DESTINY

him my recent adventures on the streets, and how I had a *hit* on my head. The way I described it must have been a bit cinematic because he said to me, "Man that sounds like a freakin' movie." The funny part about it is that it was so crazy that I didn't find it necessary to exaggerate about any of it. The fourth day I started doing push-ups and a few setups and began to feel pretty good. The back pain and the withdrawal pain were steadily decreasing. Oh, it's amazing what you can do under pressure. The fear also was beginning to decrease. Fifth day I did more push-ups, more sit-ups, and more stretching and was in a lot better shape than that first day going to that cell. The sixth day they were going to let us out and I had eventually gotten my nerve up, now I'm saying, "Where that joker at?" A far cry from that first day when I was in pain and scared to death. Almighty God must have known that I needed some time to get ready.

So the guards take us out of lock up and tell us we better cool it, and then they put us in this same holding cell which was called the *bull pen*. It was about the size of a small living room. It was a couple other the guys in there as well. I'm on one side, he's on the other side, and we both are keeping our eyes on one another. I strongly believe that the guards put us in there on purpose to see what we would do. So shortly thereafter, they take us back to D section and put me in a two-man cell on the second tier, and I think he was on a lower tier. I believe it was the next day we were out on the tiers hanging out waiting to go out in the yard, I see this one guy leaning on the rail that look like the spitting image of my first cousin *Butterball*. I stared at him for a good minute in an inconspicuous manner of course, (I know where I'm at). I walked up on him and asked him what his father's name is? Sure enough, this is my second cousin. I introduced myself to him and explained to him how we are related. We rapped for a little while and I shared with him what was going on with me. His name is Tyrone. Also, I heard that he had a little reputation that followed him from a section on the other side of the jail of knocking out a couple of guys. I told my cousin this, I said "Dig, when we go out in the yard and of course I'm going straight to the weights, while I'm lying on the bench pressing weight, make sure that joker don't sneak up on me because that's a very vulnerable position to be in."

Baltimore City Jail

He said, "Cool, I got you cuz." I noticed that the guy was walking around the perimeter of the yard as I was lifting weights. I looked to see where my cousin was, man, this young boy was running up and down the basketball court; I kept a sharp eye out for myself at that point.

At my first preliminary hearing a few months later, they offered me five years and I turned it down. Handcuffed and shackled, they took me back to my cell. While out of our cells and standing out on the tier one day, I came up with this idea. I realized that the state was offering me those five years based on that Attempted Murder charge that I had as a result of this guy. So I made the decision and walked up toward him and said, "Dig this man, I realize you and I have some unsettled business to take care of and when the time is right, we will. And I realize also that you are getting out in a month or so, right?"

He said, "Yeah."

I then said, "I have a business proposition for you if you're interested."

He replied, "What's on your mind?"

I said, "When you get out make sure you make it to my arraignment and get me off this charge, and I will nod my head to my sister to pay you $200." He said he would do it.

My mind is only on coming up out of this jail as soon as I possibly can. Incidentally, dude and I never took the opportunity for a rematch even though we had the chance to do so. I strategically redirected his thinking, knowing that he was an addict just like me. Could it be that he didn't want to risk me beating that ass? You figure, he had difficulty with me when I had him on the floor that time at 135 lbs with a dope habit. Now, two or three months later after eating and working out a little, I don't know! Anyway, I'm not sure but perhaps the potential cash coming his way was more meaningful than the sweet taste of revenge. My mamma used to always tell me, "Boy, you got plenty of sense," even though the entirety of my life up unto this point was in stark contrast to that observation. So I go back to my cell happy as I can be, because on

YOUR DECISIONS DETERMINE YOUR DESTINY

the Burglary and Illegal Entry charges, they would more than likely let me out, (only because of the ridiculously overcrowding), but not on the Attempted Murder charge.

    Another month or so later I go to my arraignment handcuffed and shackled, my sister and mother were there, and I'm expecting a good outcome. I looked around for the dude and he wasn't there. Damn! I learned later he did get out, and shortly thereafter got locked up again and was placed in another jail. So much for that brilliant plan! In the courtroom, the district attorney had showed my public *pretender* and me I mean defender, pictures of the crime scene in that room I was in. I'm thinking the pictures couldn't be that bad. I see the photos for myself, it was this big wide puddle of blood that came out of that man's head, blood all over the place, and all that I could say to myself was, "Damn." Remember, when it went down, I had to get out of there as fast as I could before the police got there. I didn't take the time to look around and assess the situation, if you know what I mean. They're standing firm with the five years to go up state and I'm still turning it down. They escort me back to my cell and now I'm starting to get a little worried about the probability of headed down to the *cut*, Jessup State Prison. The irony of it all is that I have heard a few guys that had already did state time that is now locked down in this city jail say, "I would rather be up state than spending a whole lot of months locked down in this jail." Me personally, I couldn't relate and all I kept thinking is that I didn't want to catch those five years that the state seemed to have their heart dead set on for me.

CHAPTER 20
Time to Settle In

Living day-to-day in that two man cell wasn't a pleasant experience, which obviously it's not designed to be. But you make the best out of it. In the summer, it's hot as blazes that you just have to have your underwear on. When anyone of us have to poop in the toilet, the other one usually stands and faces the bars for courtesy and to not try to smell that stink. As mentioned earlier, the jail was so crowded that at times they would just throw another joker up in your two-man cell. They would give him a little blanket to lie on the floor. That made a real tight situation in a six by eight feet sweatbox in the summer. In the wintertime, it was cold as heck in those jail cells because some of the windows on that side of the jail were busted out and they were in no hurry to replace them. The biggest relief to look forward to was when they opened those cell doors and let us hang out on the tiers for a couple of hours. Another limited relief was the chow hall and of course, out in the yard where I got my workout in.

After about four or five months in, I'm starting to adapt a little as I'm settling into this brand new reality. As noted earlier, by traditional

YOUR DECISIONS DETERMINE YOUR DESTINY

standards it took me quite some time to finally arrive to these cages, however, we adapt when we must. Then, after a couple of more months, they decided to move me to a small dormitory of about 24 men on the other side of the jail complex. Can't remember the name of this section but I do know it was right underneath the women's jail. Going to the visiting room once or twice, we would pass by them in this long hallway. They were on one side of the hallway and we're on the other side. One of those times, we turned a corner and were out of the sight of the guards for a minute. I remember pulling this woman to the side, (very willing, and cooperative) for a quick kiss and feel and not having a clue who she was. When you're locked down, you quickly learn how to steal any moment of *real life*, when the opportunity presents itself. I just wished we had more than a minute.

The entrance of the door to the dorm was a cubicle where the guards (CO's) operated from. On this dorm, the meals are brought to you on a stack of trays on wheels and there was no going out into the yard. I certainly didn't like that. Every time the meals would arrive, the guard would yell out real loud, "Feed up," a very welcoming sound for many. You were locked down 24/7 in this particular dorm. The sleeping situation was better than the cells, but you couldn't go outside of the dorm unless you were going to court or to the visiting room on another side of the complex. You would have to get creative in terms of pushups and various types of calisthenics. I was starting to get back in good shape going out in that yard and now I have to maintain being in shape however possible.

There was a small TV in the dorm, which we were allowed to watch certain times a day. I recall taking this 19 inch TV from a guy that was about to crash it on another guy's head. I told him, "Man that's the only TV we got." There were fights and beefs at times on this dorm, but we're still in jail. When you're locked in seclusion like that around the clock with a bunch of jokers, tension and tempers are unavoidable. I'll never forget, I was awakened one night,(even though you had to sleep with one eye open and one eye shut), by a real loud noise in the bunk beside me. What happened was, these two guys were fighting earlier and appeared to have squashed the beef. One of the two must have paid one of the guards to leave the bucket and the mop wringer out on the floor in the dorm after lights went out. The guy grabbed that heavy mop wringer and busted the other guy's head with it as he lay in the bunk. The guy lying in the bunk must have deflected part of the blow because if not, it would have been fatal judging by the downward force he was using. The aggressor was also looking at doing a lot of years in prison, so he probably *did* intend to kill him. I jumped up and was like, "Got damn." He didn't kill him but they had to carry him out of there. He was hurt real bad.

I've seen a couple of shanks made on this dorm. I never had one for myself but I did touch a couple of them and was reminded right away that I was locked up. Before I left what we called the steel side (cellblocks), there was an incident during our second meal. While sitting in his huge dining hall, I noticed a guy get up from the other end of the table, walked past the rear of us sitting at our table, and all of a sudden walked up behind this guy, pulled his head back real quick and stabbed him in the eye with a shank. Probably made up of a piece of plastic mirror we could get from commissary. I heard later that the guy that got stabbed in the eye threatened to rape the other guy. I have seen and heard some very foul things doing my year-long stay.

On this dorm, I met another cousin I didn't know I had. This one was a guard on the floor, on my father's side of the family. Matthew Middleton. Once we realized we were blood relatives that gave me a little relief. After being locked up for a little while, I'm now searching to connect with some type of spiritual expression. I'm not really feeling the Jesus thing my mother endorsed for a lifetime, so I think that perhaps I should try the seemingly hip and cool religion, *Islam*. My cousin was a practicing Muslim. I was interested and he brought me in some materials to read specifically about how to become a Muslim. One of the requirements was to read the first five books of the Bible. At this time, I didn't know absolutely anything about the Bible. I asked this one guy that had read the Bible for some pointers, and he obliged. I asked him about various different books of the Bible and he gave me a brief description.

So I'm reading the Bible with the exclusive intent to become a Muslim. On this section, I got into a beef with this guy and to this day, I can't remember the reason why. It was a small dorm and as I stated,

YOUR DECISIONS DETERMINE YOUR DESTINY

tensions were high at times. I do remember however, during this beef time, I had with this dude, whenever I had to poop on the toilet, I had to be in ready mode. That also went for when I took a shower; I had to keep my eyes open the whole time for fear of that joker might try to sneak up on me. I couldn't afford shampooing my hair and having my eyes momentarily shut. As I said about that woman I kissed, opportunity is the name of the game. The beef eventually died out and nothing ever came from it.

After being on that small 24-bunk dormitory, they decided to move me to the JI building. This was a larger dorm that had 100 bunks throughout the floor. A lot of guys on one floor. They often had female guards patrolling the floor late at night, which I thought was dangerous and psychologically cruel. Especially since on one end of this spread out floor was a blind spot around a corner that the guards in the cubicle couldn't see. I overheard guys planning to snatch and rape one of those female guards walking around our bunks at two and three in the morning. Especially guys that had murder charges and knew for sure that they were going to do some serious time. Even those that got caught up with that three-time loser law President Clinton implemented. It simply said that if you get arrested for the same crime three different times, you automatically get 25 years, no questions asked. I saw the faces of a few of those guys that caught that and they were not looking too happy.

I'm still reading the Bible only because that is what's required for me to start practicing to be a Muslim. After a while, my mother paid me a visit, my oldest daughter's mother paid me a visit with my baby girl that was born when I was locked up, and at that time, she was around six months old. Also, I had another old girlfriend that I went to school with decided to come visit me, twice. That was the one that I was supposed to send for when I was down in Florida. To go on a visit, you have to go all the way on the other side of the jail. I must say that when my mother came to visit me, you could see the peace on her face unlike it looked the last time I saw her showing off that 9mm. The second time she came to see me; she was so convinced that I was *saved*, it was as if she was on top of the world. She went back home and told everybody, "Stevie saved." I

Time to Settle In

decided to allow her to have that conclusion, after all, I owe her big-time. Her baby boy may be locked up, but he's off the streets and that gave her a tremendous peace.

I still wasn't too sure on which way I was leaning with the religion thing. I was first attracted to Islam, but as I kept reading the Bible, something happened to me. At any rate, I had at one time instructed my baby's mamma to kiss me a balloon filled of heroin over in my mouth during a visit. I then swallowed it. With a few crooked guards available, it wasn't difficult getting your hands on a syringe or almost anything if you could pay for it. I would have one of my buddies block the bathroom door, which had about 10 exposed toilet seats side-by-side. I would then poop the balloons of dope in the toilet, and with some thin plastic gloves that came from the kitchen, reach through the poop and feel around until I got the balloons and then rinse them off. Just a teeny bit of dope behind bars, was very valuable. And I did this without having a dope habit. This was before I experienced that born again Holy Spirit filled encounter that would bring me total peace in my surroundings. People smuggle weed, pills, and basically whatever you put a request in for, if you were cool with the right people. I used to see this kind of stuff on TV and now I'm experiencing it firsthand. I had my brother bring me a pair of new sneakers one-time and I really appreciated him taking the time to do that for me, although I knew he was a bit disappointed in me. I appreciated him coming through for me.

During one of the times when a few of us were taken over to the visiting room, shackled and cuffed, we had to pass through a few other sections to pick up other prisoners going to the visiting room. As we passed through one of those other sections, I seen a guy on the jail public phone that looked very familiar. As I looked a little closer, guess who it was? My man T, you know, the one that put that contract on my life. I came to realize that when they were giving me the chase, they evidently had orders not to shoot, but to bring me back alive so that he would probably have the pleasure in beating me to death. Reason why because a couple of those times I knew for sure that they could have had a clear shot on me, but didn't take it. As the guards kept us moving, I'm pretty sure he noticed me as well. That would be the last time I would lay eyes on this guy. I proceeded on to my visit and thought to myself, if he did recognize me, I would have to be very careful. What was working in my favor is the fact that I had been there about six months so far and already was kind of settling in and getting to know some people.

As I continued reading the Bible, something miraculously happened. Somewhere along the process of reading those first five books to become a Muslim, something overwhelmingly showed up and said, "You belong to me, keep reading." I was filled with what they call the *Holy Spirit* and had such an unbelievable peace within my spirit, that it was absolutely amazing. I literally could not stop reading the Bible. I read it morning, noon, and night. Before long, I read all the way through the Bible reading each and every book. I'm convinced that wasn't my idea or intention, I was driven and led to do that. I just couldn't put it down. Before long I started teaching Bible study in the kitchen dorm where I also lead exercise routines, since we couldn't go out in the yard.

Leadership qualities began to surface. I started getting a little fancy with my exercising by doing handstand pushups against the wall, Chinese pushups, and I saw this guy stand still and flip over backwards and land back on his feet. Aw man, that was the smoothest thing I had ever seen. I had to try it. On the first attempt, I nailed it. You couldn't tell me anything then. My teaching ability began to reveal itself at this point in time. I also started writing poetry about things that would reveal itself to me later down the road. I was so good at writing romantic poems, that I charged a few of my fellow inmates a fee for them to give to their girlfriends and wives. Eventually, the guards recognized my talent, and they paid me as well and I hooked them up too.

I remember resigning myself to the fact that if I catch these five years, oh well. Now I'm getting around 11-12 months in waiting to see what happens. Last deal they offered me was time served for one year and four years' probation, and I can walk. They carried me downtown to the big courthouse down on Calvert Street for the third and the last time in shackles and cuffs. I was released. Finally a free man and after doing a little time, I felt a bit displaced after I walked out of the courtroom. I still have this price on my head so I came up with another idea. I remember at

Time to Settle In

the end of this old 1970's movie *Super Fly* when the drug dealer wanted to get out of the drug game and the big man wouldn't let him out. What he did it was gathered a lot of incriminating evidence on the organization, put in an envelope and handed it to the DA stating that it be opened only upon his death.

The time period when I served as T's Lieut., I knew a whole lot about his operation, the various locations, and weapons stash and so on. By this time, he was back on the streets. I had a friend of mine give him an anonymous call stating that, "Steve said if anything happened to him when he come home, such as getting killed, the district attorney's office has so much information and, that it all will be released and exposed to send you away for a long, long time. He (Steve) doesn't want to have to keep looking over his shoulder, the hit that you have on him needs to be dropped. He don't want anything from you, he just wants to go on with his life." (I had him detail a couple of things so that T knew this was real). I expected him to act as if he didn't know what my man was talking about, but he knew and evidently conceded, thank you God! After nearly 12 months in jail, now I had to bargain for my life. I can't make this kind of stuff up.

CHAPTER 21

Back Up Town

So I'm back up town and have been clean for a while strictly due to my incarceration. I promised myself that I would not get a dope habit this time, which only requires me to use four or five days in a row. I didn't say that I wasn't going to get high anymore, still holding on to a reservation. I foolishly go back to the same places, around the same people and start doing the same things. Before I knew it, I not only have another drug habit, but I'm back on the streets once again, a homeless bum. It seems like what is familiar is more comfortable even when it's slowly killing me. It happened so fast as if someone changed the TV channel from one channel to another.

I managed to survive about another year with the cast of the *Night of the Living Dead* before I had to head straight back to a rehab. I would think after having been clean for a while and acquired all of that peace of mind that comes with it, even though I acquired it behind bars, you would think that I would want more of the same. Yes, I did use a few times when I was locked up, but the majority of the time I was clean. It seems like almost as soon as I got back up town, I knew it and

YOUR DECISIONS DETERMINE YOUR DESTINY

everybody that knew me was aware of the fact that I was a drug addict. I wouldn't say that I wasn't ready to stop, I just didn't have a clue about the characteristics of the *disease of addiction*, and more importantly, what it would look like for me actually to begin to recover from this terrible disease, a day at a time.

I now realize that what was required in those dynamics was the complete and unconditional surrender, being as though my problem is *spiritual* in nature. In all honesty, I'm starting to realize that I'm not there (in rehab) to get my life together but only to take a break from the madness and the insanity I practiced on the streets. After 28 days, they sent me to a recovery house and it was located 10 minutes away from where I used. I am supposed to be clean in this house but managed to sneak away several times after hustling up enough money to get a bag of dope. Still fighting and refusing to admit complete defeat. This went on for several weeks; I just couldn't stop. I was eventually asked to leave so that I could resume my madness on the streets and get out of the way of a veteran that is perhaps serious about getting his act together. Thankfully, I'm not looking over my shoulders as much but I'm still slowly killing myself just by the way I am existing. I hung out for as long as I could and as I stated earlier, streets for a drug addict are very cold. I eventually entered into another VA drug rehab at the time in my area they had about four different ones, and I been to them all, some more than once. Thank God for being a veteran and getting honorably discharged. Remember, it's a big difference between wanting to get your life together versus the need for the absence of pain.

I come out of this rehab as usual and gained a few pounds and a couple of muscles back. Every time I go into treatment, I start transforming in a couple of weeks. Drinking that Ensure twice a day and the meals that they had coupled with my workouts, I would go into an instant *beast* mode based on my prior knowledge of weight training. On to my next recovery house. This particular one located in Brooklyn, almost had me doing the right thing. Although it was completely on the other side of town from where I used, I still managed to do the wrong thing. The church that my mother belonged to was actually a couple of miles from this half way house, down on Belle Grove Road. I decided to surprise her one Sunday

Back Up Town

morning. I put on a suit and tie looking real dapper, and made it to the service. My mother was on cloud nine. She started proudly showing me off to her friends and introducing me. I sat beside her in service that day and we both were floating on air.

The food in this halfway house was fantastic and they had a little weight set in the basement. We went to a couple of AA meetings in the area and I just wasn't feeling it. Just going through the motions. Or as I like to describe it, *outwardly complying but inwardly rebelling*. I became real good at that deception. Problem is, I wind up fooling myself more than anybody else. We went to a couple of Saturday night AA dances and I had more fun than I could have ever imagined. First time that I ever went dancing without a drink or drug in my system. One day I was sitting in an in-house meeting and a guy was sharing about his father. Something clicked inside of me and I started crying profusely, and couldn't stop. One of my buddies asked me was I okay? I couldn't answer him at that moment. It was as if a water faucet handle was broken and couldn't be shut down. Later on, I realized that I finally was grieving the death of my father. Sort of a delayed reaction while I'm clean for a minute.

While at this halfway house, I somehow managed to violate my probation and had to go back to jail. This time I actually walked in to a cell without a dope habit. I was a little upset naturally, but I had to do what I had to do. I wound up doing about four or five months and I was out of there. Doing my stay there once again, I picked up the Bible, taught a few lessons as I had done before. Only problem is once I left, I wound up doing what I've always done before. Making myself empty promises that I lacked the capacity to keep. Back up town and back into the same old same old. It's as if I didn't have a clue on what to do and how to go about getting my life on track. I just couldn't grab the concept of being an acceptable, responsible, and productive member of society.

Looking back over the poor decisions I have made for my life, I've come to realize that it was all for the purpose and the plan for what was to come later. Of course, I didn't realize this divine revelation at the time. My hope for a better life had diminished to the point that I was convinced that I would die with a needle in my arm or someone

YOUR DECISIONS DETERMINE YOUR DESTINY

knocking me off for doing something stupid. Thank God, that it was all a part of a greater design. "Sometimes what you are doing right now has little to do with the present, but you're actually creating a key to unlock a door to something later in your life." I continued to exist from day to day. Only one thing and one thing in mind, how can I get some money to get my next fix. I know that my family was relentlessly praying for me, God knew I needed it.

When you are living on the streets, you try to come up with some good ideas to make your existence a little more livable. Here I go again. A couple young boys were selling heroin and cocaine in the 2700 block of Harlem Avenue. According to the streets, they had some of the best product out there. Of course, they couldn't keep the product on their persons for fear of the *jump out boys* (police) rolling up on them. It was a vacant house in the middle of the block and the front and back door was locked. It had a storm door on the front door. This is where boys would place their stash inside the storm door up against the locked front door. I'm thinking, how I can get my hands on that stash without getting caught. The locked front door had three small diamond shaped windows at the top of the door that went in a slight diagonal pattern. One of the windowpanes was broken out. One of the boys will be on the corner and the other would be near the stash waiting for the signal to get something out and serve someone. Now the stash is on the inside step up against the locked front door. I'm thinking, once I made it inside of the house, from the back balcony upstairs window, (which seems to be my usual unauthorized entrance) I needed something quiet and quick to get that stash out of there.

There were a lot of drugs in that brown paper bag. I got it! I'll set a guy sitting across the street just hanging out for my lookout. This is a guy that I use to do daytime burglaries with. His name was James and I noticed that he wasn't doing as bad as I was and he certainly didn't look like the drug addict he was. Anyway, this is the plan I hatched. He was to sit directly parallel across the street from the front door where the stash was at. I needed a lookout that I could see once I'm in the house on the other side of the locked door. There was several people hanging out in the area so he wouldn't raise any suspicion. I'm

Back Up Town

unable to see from the left or from the right what's on the other side of that door. If anyone came to the stash while I was hitting them, my partner directly across the street would just simply stand up and I would fall back. Needless to say, it's imperative that I keep my eyes on him for the signal.

I took a long hanger wire and attached it to the back of a mouse sticky pad, because I knew I had one shot at this and it had to be fast. Watching my buddy across the street, I inserted a long hanger wire with the sticky pad down through that open diamond window. Hit the bag and began pulling it up. I got so excited about this *snatch* that I took my eyes off of my buddy across the street that did actually stand up. Real bad decision! As I pulled back the drugs through the diamond window, the young drug dealer boy shouted the alarm, "Somebody is in there." Damn! I grabbed the bag and ran through the downstairs and then upstairs (the downstairs backdoor and window is locked). I went through the window I came in, jumped down off the balcony and began to run.

They jumped in their 4 X 4 and gave me chase. I wasn't in the best of shape and they eventually ran me down. I tried but just couldn't outrun a motor vehicle. They cornered me in this alley and they jumped out of the truck with their guns out asking me, "Why did you do that?"

I think my reply was, "I'm a drug addict." As if that statement was supposed to warrant some type of compassion or something.

One of the boys was literally begging his partner, "Please, please let me take him out," which is the standard response they like to do for an example. That boy was dead serious too. I found out later that the one that said no had a court date in a couple of days, thank God. I guess he didn't want to take any chances with a body being connected to him. So as I was looking at the one, very tired from all of that running, the other one took his gun, hit me across the face with it, and then held the gun pointed at me. Man, that steel hurt and he then told me that I was lucky. I go back to these same boys a couple of day later and buy some dope from them. Can you believe it? It wasn't personal it was business. With the quick money addiction they had, they weren't trying to turn any money down. As mentioned earlier, they had the best dope around. Now I'm on the streets with my nose killing me and unable to breathe through it for nearly a week.

I have one more bridge left that wasn't destroyed and this was my Aunt Pecolia. She is my mother's youngest sister and she is deeply devoted in her faith and super strong in her spirit. She let me stay with her out in Randallstown for about three or four days before I went to my last rehab. Obviously she wasn't worried about me stealing from her because I don't know if this makes any sense or not, but it seemed to be this undeniable atmosphere of strength and protection permeating throughout her home. It was deep. She clearly and confidently told me, "Stevie, you are going to be all right." I didn't see it at the time but she sure did, God bless her heart. She sent her son Todd and I to purchase a train ticket for me to go to my last rehab. Wisely, she instructed my cousin to purchase the ticket and make sure I cannot return to cash it back in. I probably would have done just that.

This last rehab I went to I was beat down and ran over like a skunk in the street. I spent 10 days in detox before I could go to the rehab part. I was in terrible shape. They had this real tough counselor there by the name of Bill Bishop. I thought he was a nut. He didn't play and although this was a co-ed veteran rehab, he would tell you in a minute to shut the f… up, in front of everybody. This cat would crush you and didn't give it a second thought. Come to find out that he didn't have more than five years clean but he did 10 years on the South Wing of the Maryland State Penitentiary and at the time, they had a reputation of beating up guards left and right. In other words, this rehab counselor would go outside and fight if you wanted to.

But you know what, despite all of that external tough shell with this guy, you still were able to connect with a passionate dude that sincerely wanted to see you get your life together. I don't know about anyone else, but I certainly sensed that belief right after he embarrassed me a couple of times when I was talking out of the *side of my neck*. He also helped me to see that I didn't have a clue about how to live. This rehab was actually a veteran's psychiatric hospital by the name of Perry Point. Part of this

Back Up Town

particular 28-day program included us feeding old World War II and a few World War I veterans their lunch and dinner meals. We actually had to sit right beside their beds and feed them their meals. At first, I didn't like it, but after a while, you develop a kind bonding relationship with these guys. One or two of them passed away during my month stay and we were very sad about that.

After I began looking human again, I started talking to this nurse and meeting her a couple times off the grounds. I told you earlier after eating for a couple of weeks and lifting weights, I transform pretty fast. I think she saw something in me. At the end of my 28 days, I had to make a decision as to where I'm going from here. Something strange and different was going on with me, unlike the other rehabs I went through. I felt a real deep hunger and thirst to get my life on track. I had two options: a mission in Delaware or a mission in Lancaster, Pennsylvania. I decided on Lancaster. One of the best decisions that I have ever made in my life.

CHAPTER 22

Finally, Redemption

>―◆―<

I was dropped off about 50 miles north of the rehab at a homeless shelter in a small town called Lancaster, Pennsylvania. I had never heard of this town neither did I know anyone in this town. I took a leap of faith by telling myself, "Whatever lies ahead for me has to be better than what was behind me." I have heard it said before that you take you wherever you go; however, I truly felt that I was bringing a *ready to change me* to this place. During that last rehab stay, I didn't know exactly what it was, but by stepping into the unknown upon completion of treatment this time, I somehow felt that my Aunt Pecolia's prophecy would come true. Never before were these particular dynamics in place. When I arrived at this homeless shelter, I hooked up with a buddy that got there a day before I did by the name of Rick who just came in from Newark. I should note that I'm finally meeting someone for the first time and getting high is not the motivation. What a change.

This particular shelter was a Christian-based Rescue Mission. As I began to adjust to this unfamiliar style of living, my number one focus was not to get high under any and all circumstances. I met a Mennonite

YOUR DECISIONS DETERMINE YOUR DESTINY

guy by the name of Mennow Fisher, who was assigned to be my Chaplain. Under his leadership, I was placed as the lead man for bringing in furniture through the warehouse and taking it upstairs in a small elevator to the Mission Store. Before we started the day, we would read out of the *Daily Bread* passage to start the morning. At first, I didn't get the significance behind this ritual, but as time went on, I began to understand the importance of starting your day with a word from God as a basis for a muchneeded spiritual foundation.

The first three months gave the mission the opportunity to load up about six of us in a van, and drive us to the Welfare Office so that we could apply for a check and food stamps. Everyone was approved. Their policy back in that day was to take 75% of your little check and allow you to keep all of the food stamps. By law they couldn't touch the stamps so with the few dollars left over after their 75% cut and the money gathered from selling the food stamps, right at the corner store across the street, there was enough to hold you for a good minute. This only lasted the first three months at which time the check and food stamps program ran out. I was totally ok with it because I was safe, clean, and had some real hope for a better life. I found out that when you are truly grateful, you don't spend too much time whining and complaining. As a result of moving that furniture around in there, we were paid six dollars a week, along with room and board, three good meals a day, and access to secondhand clothing. I was extremely grateful by comparing that brand-new reality to the hell I left behind me.

When I received my little six dollars at the end of the week, I would buy a pack of cigarettes, a soda, a bag of chips and I would be broke. The three-month welfare benefit had ended. I understood that during this phase of my life, my concerns were not about money, a real job, an apartment, a car, or none of that. My focus was allowing God to heal the brokenness that was in my spirit. To fill that great big empty void that I was previously filling with pain, misery, and insanity. As I was finally staying clean, I believed all those (normal) things would eventually come. I began to rebuild my relationship with God (that had started when I was in jail), and as a result, I considered it a pleasure whenever I had the opportunity to bless someone. Sometimes I used my imagination and

Finally, Redemption

created the opportunity to do just that. Almost the same way I would use my creativity to do something destructive. I was experiencing somewhat of a profound shift, and was liking it. A couple of those times I was even offered money for looking out for folks, and turned it down. I knew right then and there that there was truly a new me on the scene. A far cry from what I had been accustomed to. Right then and there, I sensed in my spirit that something wonderful was about to happen in my life. I thought finally, I have the chance to redeem myself and just maybe be able to start living my life as opposed to merely existing day to day. I also made a decision to connect with the Fellowship of Narcotics Anonymous. Not because I was told to do so, as I was in those various rehab's and halfway houses, but because I finally recognized my need for some immediate help in that area. That recognition, which was long overdue, seemed to have always eluded me. It quite frankly, just wasn't my time yet. I started meeting people that had what I wanted. I started becoming open to some direction other than my own. I became willing to try something new and commit to it. This gave me confirmation to a turning point in my life.

As I stayed in the shelter, before I knew it months had gone by and I didn't find it necessary to get high. God, what a sense of freedom. They did and still do, a breathalyzer check every night for alcohol after you come in, which wasn't particularly *my* twist. I joined this church by the name of *Brightside Baptist Church* and made a serious decision to *connect* with it. The same commitment I needed to *connect* to the NA Fellowship. So I started using the church and NA meetings as my direct source for accountability and spiritual growth while I was still living at the shelter. As I began to go to meetings regularly, the thought of getting high somehow was removed. I began to realize that whatever you are consistently exposed to has a direct impact on who you are. As I began to go to church regularly and get involved, that helped me to redefine myself and look at myself totally different.

I attended Bible Study every Wednesday night led by the Honorable Pastor Louis Butcher Jr. I tried not to show off when I seemed to have all the answers that were being asked in our Bible Study, but I had some knowledge. After a few classes Pastor Butcher pulled me to the side one night and to my surprise asked me what Bible College did I attend? This

YOUR DECISIONS DETERMINE YOUR DESTINY

man is very strong in the Word of God. A true visionary and soon to be led to build one of the largest church complex's in Lancaster County. To answer his question, I delightfully replied, "BCJ."

He then came back with a puzzled look on his face restating, "BCJ?"

I then broke the mystery and cleared his puzzled mind by saying, "Baltimore City Jail."

He smiled and said, "Ok." I further informed him that I was led to read the entire Bible while I was locked up and taught Bible studies. He told me then that he was very impressed with my knowledge of both the Old Testament and the New Testament.

At times when I was homeless on the streets of Baltimore sleeping in abandoned buildings, I would read a pocketsize Bible under candle light with my mind and body loaded with drugs. The spirit at war with the flesh perhaps? I confessed to Pastor Butcher that it wasn't me, but the Holy Spirit using me for that purpose. For a significant amount of time while I was using, I didn't have too much interest in having sex, especially with so many drugs consistently in my body. It just wasn't a priority at that time and as a matter of fact, if I had to choose between a bag of dope and some sex, the dope would win hands down. When I finally stopped using and all the madness that went along with it, my body seemed to come back to life all of a sudden.

I started working out again which I loved to do. I joined the Boys Club while I was at the shelter and began working out with a new buddy of mine by the name of *Champ Hall*. I opened my eyes and saw all of these pretty ladies around me, I kind of went nuts. The empty vacuum that the drugs left led me to substitute that spiritual void, that God spot. I'm learning new information in the church and in the NA meetings, but obviously I couldn't process this information fast enough to keep these new raging hormones at bay even at the ripe age of 40. I attempted to fill that empty void with many different women. I was out of control, justifying and rationalizing to myself that I was going to make up for all the lost time that the drugs took from me. In the process, I caused a

Finally, Redemption

lot of harm, broke many hearts, and made several women cry. I quickly established a reputation and I'm not quite sure if it's true or not, but I heard that they had a photo of me up on the fourth floor of the mission where the women stayed. Warning them to stay away from and avoid this guy. It probably was true.

For a while, it seemed like I was on this relentless quest, until my spirit began to convict me in such a way, that I could not continue causing the hurt and the harm that I inflicted on these different women. But there was this one young lady that I met at the shelter by the name of Dawn. She stood out in a very special way and actually captured my heart. We both seemed to have fallen for each other pretty strong. We got together as often as we could; we wrote love poems to each other that I believe were sincere from deep within our hearts, although we were homeless and broken. We used to sneak off at times where we could spend some intimate time alone together, just to be in a different atmosphere, although momentarily. It appeared that we really needed to connect with each other as we did in a very special way during a very critical point in our lives.

She left the shelter before I did and moved back to her hometown of Gap, Pa., consequently ending our short relationship. Shortly thereafter, she came back with a couple of sonogram pictures informing me, "We are going to have a baby."

Of course my first lame response was, "You sure it's mine?"

And she replied, "Absolutely beyond a shadow of a doubt."

I said, "Okay," with a deep convicted acknowledgement of, "I am the Father." She went back to her hometown and it was getting time for me to leave. They had saved a little welfare money for me to get a room, provided I had some type of employment. I found a job through this temp agency at a Foundry. I moved into my room with some basic furniture that the shelter provided me with and I began to join up with society. This job was part-time and it didn't last but a few days because in this foundry it was so hot and dangerous, I decided that it wasn't for me. Although I started feeling that, I'm finally climbing back into the ring of life.

YOUR DECISIONS DETERMINE YOUR DESTINY

The temp agency then sent me to another job boxing candy at this candy factory. This was pretty easy work and I showed up every day like I was supposed to. There were a lot of ladies that I worked with but I knew that my *lover boy* days were over. A couple of months into the job I met this pretty, dark young lady, who happened to be full time with the company. I swear that she had such an enchanting smile, that it just stayed with me hours after I had left her presence. Nothing, absolutely nothing, jumped off between her and me. Only an acknowledgment on my part, that there was something special about that girl. I would have liked to pursue something meaningful with her at the time, but I knew in my spirit that it wasn't going to happen, right then. I wasn't making much money there and as a matter of fact, I was making minimum wage, which was around five dollars and some change back in 1993.

The temp agency came to me and said that they had another job for me making $7.25 out at this plant assembling Mack Truck chassis and axles. Of course, I took the job and went out there as a temp participating in building these trucks. I was excited to be in this factory but I wanted a full-time job. I'm beginning to see myself as more than just a temporary employee. I began to value more of the way I see myself compared to the way others may see me. So every day I go to work and give it my all. Good thing I started working out regularly because this was a physical type of job. After six months on the job, the company hired me and my pay went straight to $10.88 per hour with full benefits.

I left my room and moved into a one-bedroom apartment for the first time in my entire life, by myself. I had just recently turned 40 years old. For the first year at this job, you had to work second shift of four-12 hour days. I didn't like it at first, but then I began to enjoy it. I was still consistent with the church I was attending. I started training again for competitions, and I kept going to meetings and created a pretty full life. During this time, my main high school sweetheart heard, (through my mother), that I was doing well up in Pennsylvania. Her name was Barbara and she visited me twice when I was locked up. She contacted me and came up a few times but it didn't last especially since she couldn't talk me into moving back to Baltimore.

Finally, Redemption

Also during this time, my baby girl Myiesha was born and I got to name her. You talk about a bundle of joy. She was the cutest thing ever. I used to get her, bring her to my apartment, and listen to her drive me nuts when her teeth were cutting. But, I just instantly fell in love with her. I was grateful that my job insurance paid for her delivery. Her mom and I remained friends for a longtime but were never quite able to re-ignite that strong flame we lit at the shelter. Living by myself presented its challenges. Paying the bills wasn't a problem. Learning how to cook for myself was, especially with an electric range. After overcooking, undercooking, and burning up enough meals, I had to call back home to my mother and sister to get some step by step instructions over the phone. I couldn't say that my meals were delectable, but they kept me alive. I started competing in powerlifting contests later in the same year I came to town. I arrived in January of that year and later in the fall after the shelter and getting my own apartment; I began to collect some more powerlifting trophies. By this time, I'm coming up on one whole year clean; man was I feeling good about myself.

I began seeing this one young lady and we started hitting it off pretty good. The job is coming along good; my faith in my relationship with God seemed to be getting stronger. I'm going to many meetings regularly as I'm acquiring more clean time and building healthy relationships with some men that are in my life. Two in particular are my best buddies known as Jerry and Monnie. These two guys were not only established as my road journey partners, but they also worked at the plant with me where we had lunch each and every day together for around 17 years. I'm very grateful for these two guys that came into my life and we still remain close friends over 20 years later. They taught me the importance of having some *go to* people in your life. People that you can become completely vulnerable and transparent with. Who you can share your fears, insecurities, and inadequacies and not worry about them *carrying the mail*.

Back home, I'm no longer that burden and embarrassment that I had been for so long. My family's prayers, as long awaited as they have been, were finally answered. As a result of consistently working, I began to

YOUR DECISIONS DETERMINE YOUR DESTINY

save up for an automobile. I brought an *almost brand new* Saturn that I was extremely happy to have. Drove it back home so that my family could be even more proud of me, and they were.

At this time even while I was working every day, a lot of my focus was on training and getting prepared for various upcoming competitions. From the elite training I received from my boy Clyde Wright back home, I was able to be very successful in my efforts. I mostly won first place in my category. As time went by, I would continue to get my baby girl and bring her to my apartment and just marvel over this brand new beautiful joy. She was a precious thing. I went to this National Powerlifting Competition and was so excited because they had ESPN cameras there, that I screwed up. I wound up limping out of there from injuring my leg after squatting 400 pounds, which actually was a *piece of cake* for me. But I guess the anxiety and the excitement proved a bit too much for me. This would be the first and only time I hurt myself at a competition. I recovered, and got back into action. Failures can only prepare you for success if you are determined.

CHAPTER 23
A Whole New Life

I now seem to be adapting to a way of life that I honestly had no clue existed. Sure, I saw other people living their lives, being responsible and doing their thing. But for a long time I was under the false belief that it just wasn't for me. Remember, before I even went into the Army I wasn't really trying to get down with the *being responsible thing*. Early on, it just never caught up with me. My parents attempted to guide me down that path but obviously, I just wasn't paying attention. Neither can I blame it on the neighborhoods I grew up in. The decision always rested with me. Once I got out of the US Army, it was on, non-stop and very disconnected from what many classify as *living*. It still amazes me to this day how a person can create their own reality, and live it out. It makes a lot of sense to me now. When you're lost and confused, and refuse to admit that you're lost and confused, the denial forces you to pretend and act as if you *got it together*. Although the overwhelming evidence proves otherwise. The down side to this dilemma is that you will have a price to pay, perhaps a big one.

Ok, I'm now going to work everyday building these trucks and feeling damn good about it. I'm also going to NA meetings on a regular

YOUR DECISIONS DETERMINE YOUR DESTINY

basis and starting to acquire some significant clean time as a result. Early on in my recovery, I attended this one big NA meeting that is called *Saturday Night Live*. It is a speaker-meeting format and one night I attended, I noticed a guy that looked like someone out of my old neighborhood. Sure enough, it was a guy name Mark that lived right down the street from me in the 2600 block of Harlem Avenue. We were both thrilled to see one another. I shared with him how long I have been in PA and he shared with me that he and others thought that I was dead. He had heard about the hit that I had placed on my head. News like that traveled quickly on the streets. I told him only by the grace of God, I got away. It was good to see a *homeboy* that I actually knew from the hood. He informed me that he was struggling with some serious health issues.. Mark remained in the area for a number of years and then suddenly vanished. I never saw or heard from him again after he vanished and it's quite possible that he may have passed away.

When I made the decision to join my church and become a regular member, I realized that was a strategic decision inspired by God Almighty. I continued to train at the gym. With the powerlifting experience I had, I began to seek out more competitions in different towns. I also made a decision not to allow that last setback to stop me. This sport was already in my blood. This was the lifestyle that apparently eluded me for the majority of my life. With such a full life on my plate, I continued with the decision and the newly acquired integrity to have just one girlfriend.

This particular young lady who happened to get clean around 10 years before I did, let me know in no uncertain terms that with my little two to three years clean, I basically still had my head up my butt. I wasn't really trying to hear that at the time, but with a dose of humility, she was right. One of her favorite sayings was, "More will be revealed," and it did take many more years to go by for me before I was fully able to understand the wisdom in that statement. We used to take turns visiting each other at our apartments. She suggested that I think about buying a house. Obviously, her head was further down the road from where mine was. Remember now, just a couple of years prior to this time in my life I was a homeless bum living on the streets of West Baltimore, begging for

A Whole New Life

change and at times would pick up a butt of the ground and light it up. At that point, I was extremely grateful for finally having my very own apartment. Although, the homeowner seed was planted. We continued to see each other and enjoyed each other's company.

One night I heard a knock on the door of my apartment around 9 pm. It was her in heels with this beautiful mink coat wrapped around her. I let her in and when she came out of that mink, she had absolutely nothing on underneath it. Am I in a movie? I pondered for a moment. I was blown away. I asked her, "What if you were in an accident with that pretty Cadillac you're driving?"

Her response was, "I would have been alright." Did I mention that she also went to the gym at least three times a week? One of the things that truly appealed to me about this woman is that I thought she was a class act. She had her head on straight and knew what she wanted to do. I could see that she was falling for me faster than I could reciprocate. She was a counselor and was offered a very prestigious position in South Carolina. She asked me, what should she do? I really enjoyed spending time with this lady; however, because I didn't feel as she did, I suggested that she take the offer. She reluctantly did so, and when I made a decision to fly down there one weekend, almost a month later, she still had a lot of her things still packed and boxed. She kind of pleaded with me to talk her in to returning to Lancaster. I didn't, and took that time to put some closure on that relationship. This woman turned out to be very successful as result of making that decision to move a way.

With what I had going on for me, I was very happy with my life. I was having dinner in my apartment alone one evening and I received a call from my mother. My oldest brother Gene, who had moved away from home when I was very young, was suffering with some medical issues. As time went on, he progressively took a turn for the worst and moved back home to be with his loved ones. Mamma informed me that he had passed on. At first, the bad news didn't hit me right away. But when I started thinking about him being cremated in the oven as he requested, I just broke down. Although he lived out of town the majority of my life, he was still my oldest brother and we always

YOUR DECISIONS DETERMINE YOUR DESTINY

connected when he came home at times for holidays. I missed those conversations with him. From time to time, I would visit my family and my oldest daughter Morgan, in Baltimore.

I eventually made the decision to start seeing this other young lady and we quickly got close. At this time in my life, I would never *take it easy* or the *slow down* approach as far as entering in a relationship. Didn't think taking some time to get to know you was important. "We'll find that stuff out later," I rationalized. And we did. Speaking for myself, I seem to be always motivated by sex and selfish convenience. I had some real maturing to do in that area. I'm working hard, worshipping hard, training hard, and loving hard. She attended a couple of my competitions and witnessed me building up my trophy collection. She had a small efficiency apartment and we both eventually made the decision for her to move in with me. At this point, I had lived in my apartment approximately three years by myself, an unfamiliar feat deserving recognition in comparison to my recent past.

My one bedroom apartment was a bit small for two people and it worked out only for a while. Of course, I'm continuing at regular times to get my youngest baby girl Myiesha, and enjoy just having her close by. I also would take several trips to visit my oldest daughter Morgan, back down in Baltimore. I even brought Morgan back to Lancaster a few times when she was small so that her and Myiesha could hang out and get to know each other. My little small apartment had carpet throughout and took great delight in making my girls a little bed on the floor in the living room. They seemed to enjoy it especially when I took them out to the park where of course I had already took Myiesha on a regular basis. She loved it. Stepping out in faith, we started looking at a whole lot of houses since we quickly outgrew my apartment. My credit was pretty good (only because I didn't have the opportunity to screw it up), with the exception of owing $500 to the VA for that school loan 20 years prior. When we chose a house, the real estate agent had no problem paying off that $500 debt to finalize that sale. I don't believe my mother was ever more proud of me than when I moved into my home, and neither was I.

It was a row house in the city but to me, it was like my castle on a hill. Taking some good direction from my sponsor, I made the decision

A Whole New Life

to buy this house based on *my* ability to pay for everything just on my income. Good thing too, because soon after we moved in, once again I apparently lacked the ability to commit fully in a relationship at this time in my life. She may have been the only one, but that still didn't sway me to give my all. She used to always ask me, "Why are you afraid to go all the way?" My denial would always challenge her observation. I even took her to Baltimore a couple of times to meet my family. You would think that decision would suggest a total commitment on my part, it didn't. She eventually got tired of my indecision and half-stepping and moved out about a couple of months after I brought the house. I was home alone, which was cool. Perhaps my control issues also played a part in the demise of that relationship. How does one know how good they are or what issues they need to work on unless you're in a relationship that exposes *you to you*?

Nevertheless, my life was very full and satisfying. I had everything under control so I thought, until my Myiesha's mother, decided to go on welfare. That automatically resulted in the fact that I would have to start paying child support, regardless of the money I was giving her on a weekly basis. Of course, I was already paying support for my oldest girl (Morgan) in Baltimore. I didn't foresee these changes in my income. I fell behind one month on my mortgage payment and struggled to maintain. Life all of a sudden became very real. My refrigerator was empty and my cabinets were bare. Although I had a good paying job, I didn't calculate that raised amount coming out of my check every week. A friend of mine brought over a very large pot of chili and several packs of hamburger rolls. I ate that chili each and every day it seemed like for weeks until I was able to catch up with that one back mortgage payment. To this day, I'm not a big fan of chili. But with a little help from my friend, I got through and continued living my life.

Actually, women were my least concern at this point. Whether they are in the rooms of NA, at the Health Club, on the job, or in the church, they are all around me. I can modestly declare that I'm not a bad catch. So I made a decision to be by myself for a while and focus on progressing and growing spiritually. It was time. My conscience was beginning to convict me of *living in sin* as church folks put it. I mainly focused on

YOUR DECISIONS DETERMINE YOUR DESTINY

going to work and going to the gym. I had been smoking cigarettes for around 30 plus years or so and it was time for me to stop. Even going to many powerlifting competitions I would step outside between my lifts, and light one up. Up to this point, I had been winning mostly first place trophies in my division. Like I stated earlier, the love and the passion I had developed for this sport is deep in my blood, coupled with that elite trainer I had by the name of Clyde Wright.

When I finally stopped smoking cigarettes, a funny thing happened to me. I started losing weight and losing strength immediately. It got to the point where I couldn't bench press a mere 135 pounds, a far cry down from 345 pounds. Unbelievable. I was baffled and confused. A couple of weeks had passed and I told the manager on my job that something is wrong with me, and I need to go find out what it is. He agreed because he and everyone else knew how I usually looked. When you train as hard as I was accustomed to, you can't help but look hard and buffed. I became 25 pounds lighter instantly. I heard later that rumors were going around. "What's wrong with him, does he have this or does he have that?" People will always speculate when they just don't know instead of coming to you and asking what's going on. It's not personal, that's just the nature of the beast. I went to the doctor and after a couple weeks of running almost every test in the book, they determined that I had <u>hyperthyroidism</u>. I was pitiful looking and was off from work for about a month. Understandably so, I didn't compete that year as I had consistently done the previous years.

For a while there, I was beginning to feel a little depressed after having my physique, suddenly snatched from me. I was beginning to lose hope until my faith finally started to kick in. I knew this lady by the name of Mary that had suffered the same condition prior to my experience. I sought her out because it's always comforting to consult with anyone that can relate to the trial you're going through. Tell me it's going to be all right Mary, I desperately pressed on her. She did in fact gave me some much-needed hope at a time I was going through it. Coincidence perhaps? Mary comforted me, the same name of my dear sweet mamma. I begin to think that if God allowed this to happen, He will work it out better than I could ever imagine.

A Whole New Life

So I learned through this situation how to praise God when I was right in the middle of the storm, not just when I come out of it. I made a decision not to just focus on my current reality (which was depressing), but instead to focus on the mighty power of Almighty God. I started displaying a faith when I actually had no real tangible evidence to go on. I guess that's what faith is all about. I just wanted to get back to my normal. That took quite a bit of time. I give God all the credit for all the blessings he has bestowed upon me up to this point. Even at my weakest and lowest point, I began to put a smile on my face and a gleam in my eye. I was only able to do this as a result of doing some work on that inner, spiritual man. However, it was a process.

The following year, I returned to the gym and I recall one of my gym buddies telling me that when I first came back, I looked like an *Ethiopian refugee*. I was down but not out. I learned through that experience that sometimes life can knock you down and dare you to get back up. I had read somewhere that *when it does knock you down make sure you land on your back because if you can look up, you can get up*. I made a decision to get back into the game and started training just as hard as I always did. I had a tall mountain to climb to get back where I was but as I stated earlier, it's in my blood. I had to start back off using a modest and humble approach with my training. My body weight returned and the muscle memory soon kicked back in. It doesn't take me that much time to reach a certain strength factor when I'm focused. I reluctantly took a suggestion when I got back up to par, to enter a World Class competition known as the *International Powerlifting Association*. Naturally, I was a bit hesitant, because up to that point, the highest level I had ever competed at was on the regional level and state level. I don't count that national competition where I *bombed out* with those ESPN cameras on me. There is no way I would be able to place in any of the top places. This level of competition is what my boy Clyde Wright was comfortable with. I told myself, "What the hell," at least I'll be able say that I was in a World Class competition and that would have been fine for me.

This was a four-day event held over in York, Pennsylvania. This location also boasts a unique hall of fame of powerlifters from years gone by. This is also, where they manufacture York Barbell plates and

YOUR DECISIONS DETERMINE YOUR DESTINY

ship them out from there all over the world. Just 25 miles from where I live. Previously, I had traveled hours to attend other competitions. The first three days, Thursday, Friday, and Saturday were powerlifting competitions. Some very, very strong guys and gals from all over the world attended. They were making some impressive lifts during this competition. I recall seeing one guy squat around 950 lbs. and made it look easy. I watched another guy bench press around 700 lbs. with ease. I'm telling you, these boys weren't playing around. It was as if I died and went to powerlifting heaven. The fourth day on that Sunday was the strongman competition. I see some ladies running up the hill carrying some heavy weighted wheel barrels and one pulling a van up a slight hill. "I wouldn't mess with them." I competed on that Thursday evening right after I got off of work mind you, and to my unbelievable surprise and delight, I set three National/World Powerlifting records in my weight class in the Amateur Division. I believe my edge was my age, my weight class, and my strong desire to glorify God. I was blown away. Had it captured on video and my World Record certificate is framed sitting in my dining room. The previous year as a result of my illness, I could barely lift 100 pounds. Here it is a little less than a year later I'm setting world records. God is truly amazing and this is a testament of how awesome *He* is.

CHAPTER 24

Mamma Had Never Been So Proud

I continued to do the things that were working for me such as competing, and staying connected to NA meetings and my church. As in the earlier chapters, I indicated that I needed them all. And they were working fine for me. It's amazing when you discover that once you finally stop consistently ruining your life, there is nothing else left to do but to be consistently responsible. I was feeling really good about myself while humbly acknowledging that there was no way that I could achieve this new life by myself. Before I knew it, I was stable and coming up on around 10 years free of drugs. My mamma claimed bragging rights, as she should have. This woman prayed for me relentlessly and tirelessly like you wouldn't believe. I'm aware of the fact that she constantly bombarded the throne of grace day after day and night after night on behalf of her youngest child. I am so blessed to have a mother like Mary Middleton, the finest woman in the entire world. The sheer joy of having meaningful conversations with her on the phone was priceless.

YOUR DECISIONS DETERMINE YOUR DESTINY

I got a kick out of when she used to complain about my sister Vonnie and her youngest daughter Mia, getting on her last nerve at the house. It was just the three of them there after Daddy Carroll passed away and apparently, the tension would reach an all-time high at times with these three females under the same roof. Mamma used to say, "I can't wait for Stevie to come and take me up out of this house away from you all." My God, just that confidence alone in the stability I had finally attained gave me a proud feeling unlike I have ever had before in my life. When her prayers were finally answered, I became that blessing to her instead of an embarrassment. Everybody was happy. So at times, she would call me and ask me to come get her for the weekend or so. I would drive to Baltimore and bring her back to my home in Lancaster, where she can enjoy the peace, the rest, and the relaxation she was seeking. Some trips were supposed to be just for the weekend, but I guess mamma must have said to herself, "All of that hell you put me through, I'm staying through the week."

She really enjoyed the get a way, and she really enjoyed being with me. So did I, it was like a dream come true. I would go to work every day leaving her at the house. She would just muddle around in the kitchen and watch her soap opera stories as she chilled in the living room. I felt so blessed to be able to share my home with my mother finally. The times that I had Myiesha over, I would love leaving them two together alone when I went to the gym or a meeting. Grandmother and granddaughter hanging out and having the opportunity to connect. I just simply loved it. And looking at where I came from, words cannot express completely the joy we both experienced. I had so much respect for my mamma and I was so well trained to honor her rules, that when she came to my home I told my current girlfriend that perhaps we shouldn't sleep in the same bedroom since we're not married. Mamma then quickly corrected me and said, "Oh no, this is your home."

I said, "Ok," I guess I was still a little *spooked* from the standard she maintained in *her* home. I knew she didn't play that.

While she was with me, I would take her out to the shopping mall and dinner theater restaurants for comedy shows. I wanted to show her as much as I could and do as much as I could with her. In the 12 Step

Mamma Had Never Been So Proud

Recovery process, we call it making amends. While out at the mall, mamma would walk so slow because of her health and age. I didn't mind it so much; it just gave me more time to talk with her as we moved through the mall. During one of our slow walks through the mall, I took the opportunity to make a formal amends. I said, "Mamma," with almost teary eyes, "I sincerely apologize for all the pain and unimaginable horror I put you through. You are the last person on this earth that I want to hurt and it seemed like the one person on this earth that I hurt the most. I am so sorry, could you please forgive me?"

She replied, "Stevie, I had forgiven you and I held on to the hope with my prayers that God would bring you out, you are my son and I love you." We hugged almost in the middle of the mall and I am so grateful for my mamma that words cannot adequately describe. I believe her favorite place that I took her was the *Sight and Sound Theater* where they put on various biblical plays. I took her to see the play *Noah*. The play was a bit long and near the end mamma dozed off for a minute, but she really enjoyed being there. I truly delighted in an abundance of gratitude as I watched her slip off into a short doze.

One of the times she came up, my sister Vonnie accompanied her. It happened to be one of the weekends I had a powerlifting competition to attend up in Allentown, Pa. This was the first time mamma and my sister had the chance to see me compete. We took along my youngest daughter Myiesha, and my girlfriend to the event. Mya was 6 years old at this time. I got blessed and wound up winning first place in my class and they handed me this big three-foot beautiful trophy. Judging by the look on her face, mamma had never been so proud of me. I know she was very proud of me when I first bought my home. But this single moment, I got the chance to see up close the gleam shining bright as the noon day sun beaming from her eyes. It was beautiful. Of course, we snapped a photo while we had the opportunity to capture that treasurable moment. I was just thrilled to have her and my sister watch me bench press I believe it was 330 lbs. at that competition.

It was a quality manager on my job that traveled back and forth from that area where I competed, to Lancaster. He was a member at the Gold's

YOUR DECISIONS DETERMINE YOUR DESTINY

gym where the competition was held. Although he wasn't there during the competition, he went in afterwards and told me that they had this very large photo of the officials handing me that big trophy up on the wall. I never took the time to go back and see it, but I was certainly honored by the thought of it. One of my biggest regrets was not having my father witness and experience my new life free from drugs. He unfortunately passed away about two years prior to me getting clean. Although he had his struggles as well, I can just imagine the proud look on his face seeing his youngest, finally got his act together. I did however, have the brief opportunity to make him proud the very first couple of years I started competing and winning trophies. Although it didn't last as a result of my addiction taking over, however, I'm truly grateful that some proud moments for my father did occur.

As the years passed by, I began to pull away from competing but still always in the gym. I competed about 10 years straight with the exception of that year I was sick with my thyroid condition. I actually stopped around 48 years old and that was around the time I squatted 500 pounds in a competition. I was on cloud nine. I was so hyped that night before the competition that I could barely go to sleep. I knew that I was going to set a personal record for myself in competition because I actually squatted more than that in training, however, it's in competing when it really counts because then I was a *beast*. I also still have that on video. Remember, all of my training and competing was drug-free; the natural way that I was taught by Mr. Clyde Wright in Baltimore.

I continued working hard building those trucks and was starting to feel the wear and tear on my body. I was standing on my feet and using power tools most of the day. But I enjoyed what I was doing, the pay and benefits were good and I was working with my two best friends in Lancaster, Jerry and Monnie. I gained a deep since of pride knowing that I contributed to the assembly of an untold number of Mack trucks on the road throughout the world. As a result of my church affiliation, I got kind of tired living in sin and asked God to send me a wife. The recent lady I was seeing wasn't working out that well. She had some deep issues that were revealed shortly after we had hooked up. We both concluded that this *ship wasn't heading out to sea.*

Mamma Had Never Been So Proud

At this time, my mother's health was declining and she came down with Alzheimer's. The accompanying dementia made it difficult at times for her to recognize who I was, but she remained in great spirits. Just the thought of that woman would lift me high up in the air. One of the times I went back home to see mamma I'll never forget this. She was sitting in the living room and I came in and said, "Hey baby cake, how are you feeling?"

She responded back to me in such a cheerful spirit, "I'm fine, how is your mother doing?" I admit, although I was acutely aware of her mental decline, she caught me off guard with that one.

I responded back by saying, "Mamma, you're my mother."

Then she so sweetly replied, "Oh, that's right." Then she would proceed in telling me that she was talking to her mother on the phone that morning.

I corrected her again by saying, "No mamma, grandma has been gone for nearly 10 years."

And she would reply again, "Oh, ok." That woman was the sweetest and dearest woman that ever walked this earth and I know I speak for my family as well, that she is deeply missed.

Vonnie used to tell me at times she didn't recognize her either and she was right there caring for her every day. I truly thank God for my sister Vonnie, with the assistance from my brother and nieces, for taking good care of mamma to the very end. We had a very necessary family meeting at the house in regards to the decision to place mamma in a carefully sought out nursing home. My sister Vonnie eventually concluded, "No, I will not trust my mother in the hands of complete strangers; we will take turns watching and caring for her right here in her home." She was very passionate about that decision. I felt bad due to the fact that I lived in another state and working everyday, whereas it made it very difficult for me to participate with everyone else. Eventually it fell on Vonnie and my brother Poochie who had recently retired, and he made the decision to move back in with them temporarily. It

YOUR DECISIONS DETERMINE YOUR DESTINY

takes a special kind of child to take complete care of your mother when she reach a point that she is completely incapable of taking care of herself.

Through my best cousin Byron, I reconnected with an old childhood sweetheart. She was strong in the church as well. I'm thinking about my age at nearly 50 years old, in regards to having never been married before. She was about 6 months older than I but had already been married twice. Hmm! The stronger I get into church, the more I was convicted by God's word and driven to do the right thing. So in about four or five months later, we married. Yes, I learned very soon that, that was an idiotic, impulsive decision based on pressure and guilt. It was more her idea than mine to get married that soon, however, I was a willing participant. A volunteer as some would say. The foundation was already doomed because although we knew each other as teenagers, we didn't take the time to know each other as adults.

Of course, the first year was honeymoon bliss. We both saved our money. Then we flew to the Caribbean a couple of times and took a cruise to Bermuda. During all three romantic, exotic places we visited, we argued half the time we were on the islands, about her needing to control everything. Back home, our *ship* started taking on water rapidly and it became evident real fast that this was not going to last. She decided to leave Baltimore since I already had the home and a good job further prompting the decision to live in Pa. She never quite adjusted to Lancaster.

In five years, it was over, and this Holy Ghost filled, speaking in tongues churchwoman, left a venomous trail behind by effectively and diabolically turning my precious 12-year-old Myiesha against me. She maliciously exploited the influence with my daughter that she was entrusted with and acted out a hateful vindictiveness that I have never seen before in my life. She hatefully collaborated with Mya's mother, who by all intent and signs I previously had a good relationship with, so I thought. The result was six long, painful years without any contact what so ever with my Moot Moot (Myiesha). I was blind-sided-I never saw it coming. The devil uses whatever leverage is available. I had to ask God to forgive her, I had to ask God to help me to forgive her and Mya's mom, and I moved on. Up to this point in my life, I had been consistently doing work on the inner man through the recovery process. I simply refused

Mamma Had Never Been So Proud

to allow that bitter poison to resonate in my spirit, contaminating and polluting my relationship with the real Mrs. Right, who was yet to come!

I had to put things back together again to include, re-furnishing my home, which was stripped and trashed one day while I was at work. I purchased my second Cadillac and began dating. This time I had a renewed self-image that portrayed some good, stand up qualities that I demonstrated during this marriage: fidelity, integrity, a good provider, and the like. In other words, I was a *good catch*. I then received the worst phone call that I could ever get. My brother called me and left a message that mamma had passed. I was at work and I was devastated. I went to the office with a blank numb look on my face and told my supervisor what had happened and that I needed to leave, now. I received this bad news around 10:45 that morning shortly before lunch. At first, I was going to wait until 2:30 pm when I got off. That plan and thought was completely unrealistic.

I drove down to Baltimore and joined my family in the hospital with mamma who had just recently passed. Everyone was in the room and sitting outside of the room that she was in by the time I finally arrived. This was the saddest day in my entire life. I walked into the room and saw my mother lying on the bed and her facial expression was kind of twisted as a result of her recent stroke. The lifeless body of the one woman that meant everything in the world to me was very difficult for me to process. I'm very thankful my family was there. I'm certain that fact helped ease the pain a little. It was just days ago, I was on the phone with her having an incoherent conversation due to the dementia, but her spirit was always up and cheerful. Then this sudden stroke that instantly left her brain dead, baffled and confused me. Right before I left Pa., they told me that she was still alive but hooked up to the machines that were sustaining her. I begged them, "Please, please don't pull the plug until I get down there."

When I arrived, they had already pulled the plug and my niece Tasha and my sister Vonnie explained to me that they just had to do it. Mamma's chances of coming back had deteriorated that fast. I went over and kissed her on the cheek, telling her that I loved her. God is so good that he had my family, many friends in the Fellowship, and even my job, positioned to be very supportive for me throughout this surprising tragedy. I really

YOUR DECISIONS DETERMINE YOUR DESTINY

appreciated and needed all of that support. Obviously, God knew that I would need that multitude of love to get me through. I was the youngest of the family, and I guess like most children, I boasted a special unique relationship with mamma. I'm sure none of my other siblings put her through the terror and then the pleasure by God's grace that I have. Yes, I was the starring *knucklehead* of the family. There is no one, I repeat, no one like your mother. I returned to Lancaster and pretty much resumed my lifestyle that I had been living. I thank God that I had the opportunity to write her a few nice poems while she was alive and in her right mind.

Here is one of them:

Diamond in My Eye

Here's a message to everyone in the world

About a very precious and a rare, fine pearl

Her value is priceless and there is no compare

To any other jewel around, you can go check everywhere.

This treasure is so special that it shines like the sun

I've been to the top of the world, and still could find none

After you meet her, then you could see for yourself

That what I have is greater than any man's wealth.

Yes, it's a lady I'm referring to and that I must confess

After being in her life, I know I'm truly blessed

I wish I could show one thousand ways how I love her

There is no one in this world, like my sweet mother

As God as my witness, there is none like my ma

And I will always cherish her until the day I die

What she's given me, there is no way I could pay back

I will try my best each and every day, and that's a fact.

Mamma Had Never Been So Proud

Years are still passing by and on my job, my knees are really giving me some problems. The orthopedic doctor forecasts that I would need a knee replacement later down the road. As my usual pattern goes, I was dating but nothing serious, just basically sharing time, and waiting on that *real* one. From my last marital experience, I knew beyond a shadow of a doubt, that the next Mrs. would be in for such a loving experience unlike she could ever imagine. This was so clear in my spirit from what I'd learned about myself. I sincerely asked God for three distinct things. Number one: God, you select who you want for me and how you think she should be. Number two: please give me the ability to recognize who you have chosen so I won't be looking through the lens of how I think she should be. And number three: God please teach me how to love her in the way that you love me. In the fullness of time, God released one of the very best Angels he had living in his kingdom with him. When God knew I was ready, he sent her down from heaven on the wings of the wind straight to the center of my heart.

CHAPTER 25
Angel in Disguise

Now keep in mind that I first met this lovely woman 16 years ago when I took a temporary job at this candy factory, the very first year I came to town. She was one of the cutest chocolate girls that I've ever seen. She had an enchanting smile that would stop you right in your tracks, but obviously, that wasn't the time for us to connect back then. During the course of those many years, we would see each other in passing and cordially speak to one another. The smiles would be there and that was always as far as it went. Probably because I was seeing someone at the time and so was she. We would see each other in the grocery store at times and I myself would walk away with what seem like a pleasant cloud lingering in my head. I didn't know what it was at the time, but I remember thinking that there is something uniquely special about this lady. She shared with me later that during a couple of those times in the grocery store she wanted to reach out and touch my butt, I didn't know that. The decision to maintain restraint on both of our behalf's was apparently necessary for what was to come.

When the time was right, we ran into each other at the deli in the rear part of *Giants*, and wow, did we make a connection. This time we spoke directly to each other with more conviction and with the expectation of a call from destiny. She asked me was I married. My response was, "You don't see a ring on my finger, do you?"

Of course, her response was, "No, I don't." I then nervously asked her for her number. With a bit of excitement in her eyes, she gave it to me and I promised to call her that night. Before we had left the store she went down to the dairy section of the store and shared with me later that she prayed that I would follow her. Well, God apparently heard her prayers because I definitely followed her after I got my deli order; I proceeded in that direction just for the hope of getting one more glance at this walking dream. I was just so excited and so thrilled with the hope of getting close to this fine, sweet lovely woman.

When I left the store, I had a few other errands to run. I couldn't wait to make that call. This would be the most anticipated call I would ever make. So I finally made it back home and got comfortable. This was *the* phone call of a lifetime. When I opened my phone and searched for her number, it wasn't there. Oh no! I went into panic mode. I just couldn't believe that I forgot to *save* the phone number of this one lady I wanted to get to know more than anybody on this earth. The excitement and thrill of the moment when I first got her number must have thrown off my concentration. I didn't quite know what to do. All I knew that my mistake was completely unacceptable. One minute I was flying high in the clouds, and the next minute it seemed like I fell back to earth with an uncertain crash.

At this time, a family lived directly across the street from me that grew up in this town, as she did. I described her as best as I could to this one guy over there on his porch and he immediately knew who I was talking about. I was so relieved. He told me exactly what street she lived on but didn't know the address number. Good enough! So I made a decision to drive up that one-way street looking for a little white car that she was driving. I had no luck. Didn't know at the time that she had the car parked around back. I just couldn't believe that I came so close to the girl of my dreams and didn't save her phone number. I was very upset with myself but still remained a bit hopeful.

Angel in Disguise

One Friday evening after I got off work I decided to go to my favorite store, Giants, and take *that* particular route with the lingering hope that I might see her. I happened to be talking on the phone to a lady friend while I was driving, and when I reached the stop light on the corner of Church and Vine Streets, guess who walked just a few yards from her house waving at me? My Angel in disguise. I beckoned to her to let me park on the other side of the traffic light. At this moment, whoever it was that I was talking to on my cell phone all of a sudden became truly insignificant. I acknowledged her with an exciting wave indicating that I will park as soon as the traffic light change. I anxiously crossed the green light and pulled over to park up a little way on the same side of the street that she lived on. This day would officially connect me with the true love of my life.

I got out of my car and walked back down to the front of her house. Actually, she was having a conversation with her Aunt Renae who is someone that she's very close to. I walked up to her cool and anxious at the same time. She extended her hand out and I immediately grabbed her and held her tight telling that her I don't shake hands, I hug. I smelled a little alcohol on her breath when I hugged her and remember thinking, "Oh no, I have a drunk on my hand." Thank God, that thought was completely inaccurate as I found out later. I overreacted being as I'm still in recovery. She asked me why didn't I call her and I explained to her that I unintentionally did not save her number in my phone.

She didn't say it, but I believe her reaction to that excuse was, "Yeah, right." I asked could I see her later and it seemed like we both were very excited with wonderful expectations.

We didn't meet up that weekend, but the following week I went back to work with a smile on my face and a glow in my heart that revealed, something was going on with me. She also went back to work looking different because she told me that one of her close co-workers asked her one question when she came back to work. Who is he? Funny thing about this connection is that she also told me that she had already told her family and friends about me a whole year or two before we actually made a connection. In other words, our union was placed down in her

YOUR DECISIONS DETERMINE YOUR DESTINY

spirit before it manifested in our life and that blew my mind. I was blown away with that early on foresight that she had about her and I. I had never experienced anything like it before in my life.

One of the very first times I paid her a visit, I was supposed to be there around 8 pm and got tied up doing something else and didn't call her to say I would be late, I didn't think it was a big deal. Well, when I arrived there an hour or so late in the rain, she told me she didn't want to see me. I said to myself, "This chick has a lot of nerve telling me no this early on." Nevertheless, I respected her feelings and regrettably went back home. I later told her with a spirit of pride that she was lucky I gave *her* another chance. Really? The next time I paid her a visit I was a bit nervous and I'm sure she was too, however, we set down and watched a little TV and began to talk. Right away, it was very obvious that this was going somewhere.

We continued to see each other and it was just impossible to avoid falling in love with each other. You can't stop a runaway train no more than you can stop the falling rain. As the weeks went by, we seemed to understand that we were simply created for each other. Now we all know that when two lovebirds first get together it seems like music floating around in the air. I just knew in my heart of hearts that this was a deep, intuitive, spiritual connection that just simply could not be denied. Weeks began to turn into months. By this time, we both are notifying all of our friends and family members that we had found the greatest love of all time. I made a decision to take her to Baltimore and meet my family. One of my young cousins was getting married and I was so proud to introduce my lady to my family. You can tell right away when that introduction to your family kicks off good, and it did. Good people always connect with good people.

Back home, we took turns meeting at her house and meeting at my house. She had started complaining about not seeing me enough times on the weekend. So I decided to take her to Baltimore once again to the City Zoo. By the time we reached Baltimore it was closed. Considering myself as one as being good at thinking on my feet, I activated my plan B and took her to *The Great Blacks in Wax Museum* in East Baltimore.

Angel in Disguise

The only one of its kind in the entire country. She was not only impressed with the museum, but evidently, we had fallen in love with each other so fast and so strong that it was clearly destined to be. As we made it around inside the entire exhibit, being as though we were newly in love, I couldn't keep my hands off of her and she didn't mind one bit. It was obviously clear that we were more into checking out one another than the unique exhibits that were on display.

After we left, I drove her to West Baltimore and we ordered something to eat from this restaurant on the corner of Edmondson Avenue and Franklinton Road. While we were standing outside waiting for the food to be done, once again, we were simply all over each other in broad daylight. It must of have been a little contagious because it was a younger couple that approached the entrance of the carryout arguing a bit. Once they went in, placed their order, came back outside, and noticed Cherry and I just showering love on each other, their encounter soon turned from agitation to loving affection as well. We just couldn't help ourselves and this marked one of the many unforgettable moments that we shared.

When we returned to Lancaster, she wasn't too sure of whether I was going to drop her off or come in with her, or take her to my home. I had initially told her that because I see this as something super special, I didn't want to press too hard too fast. In other words, I didn't want to anxiously screw this up and scare her off. To her much delight and my exquisite pleasure, I brought her to my home for the remainder of the weekend. As the months passed by while her and I continued acting like high school sweethearts, we began moving toward nine months to be exact. I asked my sweetheart a question. "How would you like to go to Jamaica?"

She was like, "Are you serious?"

I said, "Yes, I always wanted to experience that island with someone that I could share every moment of love with in the Caribbean." I told her all you have to do is pack a bag and be ready to go. She was very excited because obviously she was never offered that type of opportunity before I came along. I also never offered this opportunity to anyone either that I wasn't married to.

YOUR DECISIONS DETERMINE YOUR DESTINY

You have to understand, what Cherry and I were experiencing superseded any and all legal or formal doctrines of a relationship. No one but Almighty God was making all of this happen. I don't think that she was thoroughly convinced until I took her out to the travel agency at the mall and paid for the trip. I actually invited her in to help decide which package we should take. Looking at her face in that moment you could clearly see her revealing an expression questioning, "Is this really happening"? After that, she went back home and called everybody she knew sharing the exciting news with them, "I'm going to Jamaica." We got our passports in order, packed our bags, and headed to the Tropics.

We caught a break at the time we went out to pay for the trip. There was a brand new 5 Star adult resort just opening (Secrets) and they had an incredible opening promotion deal for 7 days. Perfect timing. Needless to say, the seven days we spent together on that island was nothing but pure paradise. You wouldn't believe how much we had done in one week. One night in particular we were walking around the resort holding hands and the best way I can describe that moment is experiencing a feeling that you have dreamed about all of your life. It's almost indescribable, later that same night we were in the pool, just the two of us under the romantic Caribbean moonlight. I will remember and cherish those moments for the rest of my life. The poet that I am, motivated me with great inspiration to capture that experience in a piece I wrote aptly named:

Paradise

Standing face to face, illuminated by the fluorescence of the Caribbean moonlight, in a shallow patch of Jamaican beach. Our eyes penetrating each other like an instant surge of lightning bolts. Feeling so close in this exotic comfort, as close as the layers of our skin. Knowing that all of this wonderful pleasure around us almost comes as close to the deep river of love that pours out of us. A single moment more thrilling than any event in history. Captivates us, stills us, and then flys us to the highest height of ecstasy. The combination of you and I and our opulent surroundings epitomize one of the most sought after experiences throughout time. No, we're

Angel in Disguise

not in heaven yet but it's sure difficult to distinguish this from that. Ever since you walked out of my dreams into real life, every day has been filled with the thrill of excitement. I waited for you to come along for such a long time and then one day, heaven smiled on me. So since my love is certified from above there is no way that I will ever return this precious gift of YOU. Ahh paradise, true paradise. Is that distant geographical haven? Not exclusively, because when we are walking down the aisle of the grocery store holding hands like high school sweethearts, in the twinkling of a moment we seem to be zapped right back to the island of Montego Bay. Which led me to a startling revelation: It's not just where you are, but who you are with and the romantic landscape you have deep down inside of you.

We returned from the trip and some people thought we may have gotten married while we were away, a fair assumption based on the way we were always acting with each other. We wanted to, we even met a preacher lady and her husband that was on vacation there that offered to marry us, but it was too soon yet. I had learned from my previous mistake.

When we came back home, our love for each other continued to grow and get stronger. Seeing each other on the weekends and sometimes one or two days a week, was not enough for the both of us. We both are working full time and are eagerly ready to make some adjustments. One day she was lying on my couch watching TV in my house and I said to her, "Look, I need to see you more days that we are currently doing." To my surprise, she was on the exact page as I was and began *quietly clapping her hands* as a gesture of complete agreement. So we both decided to spend a few more days through the week together as well as the weekends while taking our time and not jumping too fast. The following year I asked her to move in with me and she graciously agreed. Never was I so happy before in my life.

As we began to get comfortable living together, about a year and a half into our relationship, she shows me this engagement/wedding ring

YOUR DECISIONS DETERMINE YOUR DESTINY

downtown that her heart was set on. We were just out and about walking around downtown enjoying one another's company. Little did she know, I went back to the store and purchased that exact ring. While she wasn't looking, I placed it inside of a flower bowl on the coffee table in the living room. She was sitting on the couch talking on the phone to her sister Barbara in South Carolina. I asked her to put the phone on speaker as I assumed a kneeling position and I hit her with this,

"For many years I have waited for someone like you,
To come along and show me what real love can do.
Since the beginning right from the very start,
You came and captured the title to my heart.
I saw you fly down from heaven on the wings of wind,
Not just to be my true love, but to be my best friend.
Yes, I know I'm truly blessed for the rest of my life,
But there's one crucial thing missing my love,
Will you please be my wife?"

I then produced that ring that she fell in love with. Her sister and her brother-in-law heard the proposal as well. My sweetheart was so excited when I produced the ring that she wanted; she forgot to say yes until her sister informed her that she didn't give me an answer.

Then she said, "Yes, yes, yes," and we set a date.

CHAPTER 26

Knocked Down, But Not Out

Now here is where things begin to get a little tricky. I had been on my job for over 17 years. Assembling Mack Truck chassis can wear you down over a period of time. My body wasn't quite able to keep up with the truck parts that I was assembling. My knees were really giving me some problems as the years went by. It wasn't until the last couple of years of my employment did we finally get the opportunity to implement a Union, to the company's displeasure. We were not fighting for more money necessarily, but better work conditions and reasonable benefits. Naturally, the management to include the president of the company went to great lengths to try to dissuade the employee's efforts to establish a union, with no success. With long drawn out negotiations and with the company and union officials bargaining, they reached a very reluctant agreement. To insure that agreement, we had to go on strike in front of the factory a few times and one of the times, the local TV news station covered it. I was even able to see the few seconds' coverage of us

YOUR DECISIONS DETERMINE YOUR DESTINY

striking and myself proudly displaying my strike sign on TV news at my home when they aired it.

Every one of the full-time employees that joined the union had a *bull's eye* target on their back. Major lawsuits brought against the company would result in fines and costs ranging in the millions before the company was eventually ran into the ground. It turned out that this particular outfit *Lancaster Preferred Partners* that brought out the original *Dana Corporation* was corrupt and unscrupulous. One by one, the company began to systematically eliminate those targeted full-time employees, (such as myself) and replace them with temporary agency employees. I came back from lunch one day and the supervisor asked to speak to me in the office. I knew what was up and replied to him, "So you going to fire me now, huh?"

He said, "No no, we just need to talk." Didn't even have the integrity to get honest with me, even at the end.

So he sat me down with the Quality Manager, the HR manager, and himself. They then proceeded to fabricate and justify the need to terminate my employment. I just sat there not saying a word while allowing them to go through the motion of what the president directed them to do. Odd as it may be, when the HR manager was asked to escort me to my car in the parking lot, (which is the custom), she was almost in tears deeply regretting being a part of that injustice. Over the years, we had established a nice relationship, her, and me. I tried to calm her dismay by confidently letting her know that my God is in control of my life, not this company and I will be all right. I really didn't know what would happen and how exactly I would be *all right*, but something in my spirit seemed to let me know. So I made the decision to console this lady who was reluctantly a part of my termination. In other words, I decided to be spiritually generous as opposed to being bitter and resentful. I truly believe that because of that particular response to that trial in my life perhaps that set the course for my next blessing to come.

I have strengthened my faith over the years and the test of my faith was called up on stage. I pulled away after all of those years, actually grateful and expecting God to move in a big way on my behalf. Reluctantly, I then called my fiancé Cherry, and told her what happened. Her response collaborated with my spirit by her saying to me, "Honey, we will be all right." I really don't mind saying that her words were very encouraging and much needed at that moment. Because when you're current reality drastically changes, it could very well throw you for a loop. We were living together at this time and she was working at a job that she had for a number of years as an Insurance Claims Adjuster. We did get married just 6 months after that unfortunate ordeal; our heavenly ordained love would be undeterred.

Now I really had to put my faith to the test. I offered my sweetheart a choice, "Would you like to have a nice size wedding and invite everyone, or would you prefer to go to the Justice of the Peace and fly back down to the Caribbean for our honeymoon?" I believe it took her less than one minute to decide. I guess after having a dynamite time in Montego Bay, that she wanted more of the same. I allowed it to be completely her choice since now we have to be prudent with our finances. So we booked a week trip and went to the Dominican Republic for our honeymoon. An unbelievable experience for both of us. It was as if we flew into our very own slice of Heaven.

The resort we chose was excellent in every sense of the word. It was an adult only resort, once again. The nighttime entertainment almost rivaled a smaller version of Las Vegas. To top it off, our room was right next to this beautiful waterfall that ran into our *swim-up pool*, perhaps just 10 ft. from our back door laid out with a couple of lounge chairs adjacent on both sides of a little walkway straight from the door to the edge of the pool. Words can't adequately describe this exotic honeymoon that we experienced in Punta Cana.

The seven days that we were in Jamaica that year before, we went out on many excursions: *Zip Lining; Catamaran Booze Cruise* boat, which allowed us to swim in the Jamaican Sea; *Dunn's Waterfall Climb*; *Glass Bottom boat* ride; and *Canoe Rafting* through the river way. We stayed busy in Jamaica. However, when we went on our honeymoon to the Dominican, we didn't leave our resort to go anywhere and we didn't

YOUR DECISIONS DETERMINE YOUR DESTINY

need to. I asked my new bride did she regret not having a big wedding instead of coming here. She said, "Not for a minute." We brought back some great photos and videos to capture this once in a lifetime dream experience. Now back to reality.

Naturally, I filed for unemployment compensation, but was denied. Although I was told the contrary when I left, the company chose to deny my claim. That was unacceptable to me and so I decided to appeal that decision. Work Quality was supposed to be the issue of my termination, although I repeat, I consistently did this work for 17 years. While I'm waiting for my appeal date, it so happened that a coworker friend of mine (Big John), who was also terminated prior to my firing date, worked as an Inspector on the line. For some reason he held on to a thick stack of quality reports to include the area that I worked in. God is so good. What those reports revealed was that my quality discrepancies were at such a bare minimum, compared to the rest of the line that it was very clear to see that my termination was not justified, to say the least. I give credit to God for seeing in advance, what I would need. With the overwhelming and irrefutable evidence I presented, they approved my claim and paid me for several months back.

My right knee was hurting me so bad that I started to walk with a limp. I can't have that because that limping was interfering with my *swagger*, if you know what I mean. I was constantly in a lot of pain. They had told me three years back that when the cortisone shots completely stopped giving me relief, I would eventually need a knee replacement. I made a decision to allow the VA to do a knee replacement on my right knee. It was just too painful and the quality of my life was deteriorating as a result. I went in for surgery that day weighing exactly 202 solid pounds because I knew that I would be laid up for a while and I wanted to be a little heavier and solid than usual, and I was. Six days later as a result of my knee replacement operation, I was sent home weighing exactly 173 pounds. I was devastated. That's nearly 30 pounds lost in just one week.

What had my immediate attention was the challenging post knee replacement process. It was very painful, but I was determined to get back up. I was knocked down but not out. Because of the strong pain

Knocked Down, But Not Out

medication I was on, I had absolutely no appetite. I thank God that my wife was there for me, hand and foot. I'm pressuring the doctors to get me back to my weight gain as soon as possible, and those knuckleheads were clueless. You forget sometimes that doctors are just *practicing medicine*. I'm getting furious because I'm used to looking and feeling a certain way. Although I stopped competing some years ago by now, I still quite frequently workout to maintain a certain standard of being somewhat *buffed*, it's in my blood.

As my right knee began to heal and become functional, my left knee is now killing me because of the overcompensation. Reluctant as I might have been, I needed it done as well and made the decision to go get that one done also. I cautioned the same surgeon about what happened with my weight loss as a result of this process and he asked me did I want to hold off. Absolutely not. I need both of my knees functioning properly. I have things to do. The healing process was a bit difficult for me. Having strong pain narcotics in my body after 20 years without having any drugs in me, was a shock I don't think my body was quite prepared for. It was rough. Five or six months passed by and my weight is still down. I recall my primary doctor saying to me, "Well Steve, maybe this is your new normal."

My reply was, "I don't mean any disrespect Doc, but you must have lost your Got Damn mind." Yes, I told him just like that. I don't allow other people's opinion of me to become my reality. Not even a so-called professional. I was fed up with them because not only were they unaware of what happened, but also unable to get me back to where I was. I was knocked down, but not out.

Naturally, I stopped working out and attending meetings as well as church. I was house bound for at least the first month. Slowly but surely I began to get a little mobile and eventually made it back out of the house, with my walker. The rehab process was slow and painful but I was determined to push on. I had a buddy come pick me up and take me to a NA meeting. While at a NA meeting, I meet this brother from Baltimore by the name of Kevin. We didn't know each other in Baltimore but we hung out and ran around some of the same areas. As we were connecting, I asked him did he know a certain drug dealer that went by the name of *T*.

YOUR DECISIONS DETERMINE YOUR DESTINY

He said, "Yes as a matter of fact he had brought drugs from him." I then disclosed that he had put a contract on me for robbing him. Kevin then replied, "You don't have to worry about that joker anymore, someone *took him out.*" We then both concluded, "You live by the sword, you die by the sword."

My wife suggested that I go to another specialist within the VA system to get another opinion and a different perspective on this dramatic and traumatic weight loss. Perhaps in another town because my suspicion was that somewhere in the process of the surgery, they threw off my *thyroid gland* that as you recall, I had an issue with many years ago. But they are telling me no, that was not the issue, but still not offering me a pathway back. So I go to this other thyroid specialist at a different VA facility over in York, Pa and she tells me something different than her colleagues have been telling me. She told me what to do, set me on my path back and within a month I gained all of my weight back. My wife also suggested that I file for Social Security Disability. A little hesitant at first, not because of the unemployment I was receiving, but because I just didn't think I could get it. Upon her suggestion, I filed the claim while my knees were still healing and in two months record time, they approved me. I did have other medical conditions going on as well. My wife is a very smart woman. They backed my claim to the time I was terminated simultaneously becoming disabled and paid me *10 big ones* even before I received my first monthly check. I was like; you've got to be kidding me. Listening to my wife proved to be very wise, indeed.

You think that's all? Ready for some more? Pres. Obama approved a tuition assistance program called VRAP (Veterans Retraining Assistant Program) for some that will qualify. I was in my late 50s now and hadn't been to school in a long, long time. I had just barely made the age requirement (under 60) and got in at the right time before the Republicans pulled the plug. This particular benefit didn't last no longer than three or four years. Was I lucky or was I favored? The offer was if you enroll in a two-year college degree, for the first year the VA would pay you a substantial amount per month for 12 months. I couldn't refuse that offer. At first, I'll admit that I felt a little guilty collecting income from these three different sources. I even asked my wife, am I doing something wrong? When I filed for my unemployment, I did in fact put down that I was available for work, with conditions. At the end of the year for IRS purposes, they of course were fully aware of all the income I was receiving, but no issue.

I believe that my timing couldn't have been more perfectly ordered. I was on Unemployment for (32) months. That extension option will probably never happen again. How can I not feel highly favored and truly blessed? During school, I struggled with some of the classes at first, especially Business Algebra and College Algebra but I persevered. Some of my classmates were young enough to be my grandchildren, but that didn't stop me. I have come to learn that when something that is in front of you that is pulling you and is stronger than what's trying to keep you back, you really don't care who's around you and what they are saying about you. Destiny was calling. I completed the school and received Associates in Science in my chosen field, with honors. Now my true motivation for going back to school at that late age in my life was strictly for the money, *so I thought*. But God used that money as a *carrot* for me to bite on so I could operate in a plan that he had for my life.

When I lost my job, after all of those years I truly didn't know in what manner God would bless me, but I just knew that he would. I have heard before that God will use what someone intended for your harm, and turn it around and let it work out for your good. I'm also a firm believer that when you are chosen to carry out a divine purpose, can't no devil in hell stop it from happening. We have seasons of plenty when you're high on the mountain top, and we can have seasons of lack when you're down in the valley. At this time, I'm not only riding high with abundance, but I made a decision to store up some of that harvest in the barn so that when the famine comes, we'll be a little prepared. This abundance I'm talking about is not just limited to money, but also health, friends, and even peace. Even at this point, when I look back over my life and I see the times when I should have been dead, I see the times when I could have easily lost my mind, I can only stop and say, oh what a mighty God I serve.

CHAPTER 27

How Bad Do You Want It?

As time goes by, I'm continually doing very well and things are just moving right along. Thank God, I have been obviously making some good consistent decisions. Next thing I realize is that I have been clean for 20 long years. Wow, simply amazing.

Can you believe it based on my past? How I struggled trying to survive, longing to climb into the ring of life. This is celebration time. My wife and I made a decision to plan a party in my honor to recognize this great milestone. Her and our oldest, Reese, put some delicious food together to serve the many guests coming to help me celebrate. We ordered a beautiful velvet cake with a picture of me going to my last rehab indicating the year of 1992 and a current picture of me buffed up in the year of 2012, what an amazing cake. When a lot of the people saw this cake, all they could say was *wow*. My friends here in Lancaster as well as my family from

YOUR DECISIONS DETERMINE YOUR DESTINY

Baltimore came to this festive occasion. I rented a hall in Lancaster on Columbia Avenue to facilitate the party.

I hired a DJ to play some good music after the honor recognition tradition, by the many that attended. It is customary that when we celebrate a 20 year milestone by having a party, the honoree takes a seat in the middle of the floor and a variety of people grab the microphone and give honor and praise based on their relationship with the honoree over the years. I guess you can call it a special type of *roast*. One of the things my wife and I were greatly anticipating was at least a dozen of men and women giving honor and gratitude to myself in the company of my family. Remember early on how I terrorized, embarrassed, and was a burden to my family for quite some time. Although my mother wasn't present, God bless her soul, my sister, my brother, my daughter Morgan and grandson Ricardo, my nieces and nephew and family friends were all there.

One of the recognitions stands out in particular was from my sister. When she grabbed the microphone, first thing she said with almost teary eyes was, "My brother should be dead," with heartfelt gratitude. She also recounted how she watched my mother pace back and forth in her bedroom, night after night with her Bible in her hand praying, "Lord, please don't take my son." I had no idea of this relentless pleading my mother displayed on my behalf. She and the rest of my family had a front row seat to the madness and insanity that I lived out year after year. Not to mention that time when a total stranger came to her door promising her that when he saw me, he would kill me. At the time, I was completely unable to stop and comprehend just for a moment, the depth of horror I took my family through.

My brother Poochie grabbed the mic and remorsefully apologized for any part he played in being a negative influence in my life. I tried to assure him that he couldn't corrupt what was apparently destined to hit the bottom of the sewer. In other words, what I went through and the decisions that I made were a passageway for me on my way to my destiny. *I* perhaps should have been the one to apologize for the negative part I played in *his* life. In fact, my brother was a great example for a role

How Bad Do You Want It?

model to look up to ever since he came back from Vietnam. During his probation officer career for the State of Maryland, he would often stop by my mother's house at lunch time for a sandwich or perhaps a slice of mamma's famous homemade cake. This was at an earlier time when I was living in the basement of my parent's house as I often did for several years. This one day Poochie stopped by for lunch with his customary suit and tie on. We had just shared a small bag of drugs down in the basement. When my brother went back upstairs in the kitchen where mamma was, the drug *hit him* in such a way that he completely froze up like a mannequin. To his credit, I'm sure I would have experienced the exact same effect except my body was so used to drugs in it that it didn't bother me as much. Mamma was super furious at me. She yelled back down the basement, "Stevie, get up here." I came up the basement stairs to see what was going on and she immediately blamed me for what was going on, and understandably so. I can imagine her concern and fear due to the fact that I wasn't doing anything constructive with my life while my brother had it *going on*. I might pull him down to my level was obviously the fear she had. Thank God, that wasn't in His will. He put a cold rag on his face and he soon came around. I felt real bad about that and mamma *laid me out* real well after he left and went back to work. That's one of the reasons why I should be the one to apologize instead of him apologizing to me.

My favorite niece Tasha grabbed the mic next and recounted when she was young how she used to sit on the basement steps and watch me lift weights (before it all went bad). When she was very young, she truly loved her uncle and told me that she wanted me to be a policeman. *Fat chance of that*! Many friends got up and spoke very highly of me and my family told me shortly after that they were simply amazed at the impact I had with so many people. When a group of people take time out of their schedule and travel some distance to honor *you*, it's a very humbling experience. I was so proud and thankful at that moment, that words cannot adequately express my true sentiment. For me, the highlight of it all is when my wife took the microphone and shared our story of how we got together. She also stated, "*Steve* is a great man whether we were together or not." My wife has a very unique and genuine way of detailing our inevitable destiny. I must say out of all the compliments and

YOUR DECISIONS DETERMINE YOUR DESTINY

praises, I was receiving that night, that one was the *show stopper* for me. After much other personal recognition, I signaled the DJ to get the party started. Everyone that attended was greatly appreciated for participating in this monumental event of my life. We ate some very good food and we danced until it was over.

Now with this college degree sitting up in my living room for a showpiece, I really wasn't that motivated to use it. As I stated earlier, my intentions were not to launch a new career in my life at the age of 59. However, my spirit began to convict me because I wasn't fully operating in the *gifting* I was assigned. In other words, I felt that I wasn't living out my purpose or even coming close to it. And I clearly knew this. Our bills were getting paid and we would take out vacations usually in the tropics, however, something inside of me was unsettling. So I began to apply for a counseling position at various facilities. A couple of them told me that I didn't meet the educational requirements but I refused to be dismayed. One other place I applied to was a center that helped drug-using teenagers and counseled their parents at certain times. The director that ran this organization, another guy by the name of Steve, decided to give me a trial run by allowing me to set in on a few group sessions. Honestly, I just wanted to observe this unfamiliar process. I was asked for my input towards not only the troubled youth, but to their parents as well.

The results were that I was obviously connecting with the clients so well, (by their own admission) that I unintentionally overshadowed the director's input. He and I were very similar in many ways but through my unique experiences and my ability to connect spiritually, I sensed just a little bit insecurity. I could only sense that I was more effective breaking through to the clients and their parents that it became too obvious who perhaps, should have been in the lead. God knows, I wasn't trying to show off but I was just motivated to help in ways that I'm apparently gifted in. However, that brief experience revealed to me that I have a gift fueled by a God given passion to connect with broken and confused individuals seeking help. We discussed a comparable salary and a proposed start date. I had a feeling that it wasn't going to happen, and it didn't.

How Bad Do You Want It?

As I was holding back all of the knowledge and experience that I had gained, I began to experience some blood in my stool. I wasn't too concerned at first until it consistently showed up when I had *to go*. Finally, I made a decision to go get checked out. After about three different colonoscopies over a period of four months, I was diagnosed with ulcerated colitis, a bowel disease that has no known cure. I had no idea of the living nightmare that lay ahead for me when suffering with this particular condition. It had become so bad that I had lost a lot of weight once again, but more frightening than that was losing the ability to control my bowels. I had a lot of accidents before the doctor was able to get it under control. I was housebound for about a month out of fear of having a guaranteed accident. During that month, I had to be real close to the toilet at all times, that's how bad it was. Once your *colon* or *large intestine* becomes inflamed or otherwise termed as *ulcerated*, you can have a bowel movement and not even be aware that you did, until something don't quite smell right. My poor wife was a tremendous help to me once again in dealing with those flare ups in a way that I will forever appreciate. She tirelessly assisted me in ways that could have only been motivated by love. I thank God for my Angel in disguise daily. They eventually got me stable again and developed a plan to maintain my stability, so we thought.

So the unemployment eventually ran out as well as the VA monthly checks I was receiving. I'm down to one income and although my dear wife is helping out, things are getting kind of slim contrary to the lifestyle we both became accustomed to. At the same time, my second Cadillac that I had for nearly 8 years was starting to give me some serious problems. So I stuck with the decision to continue looking for some type of counseling work because at this stage in my life, factory work is just not *on the table* for me anymore. One of the last jobs I applied for was at that very same homeless shelter that I was dropped off at 22 years earlier. It also happened to be right in back of our home. Approximately 2-3 hundred yards from our backyard fence. Literally, this job is around the corner. I dropped off my resume and a written account of my spiritual journey, as they requested. They gave me two interviews. The second interview was with a supervisor and two life coaches. One of the life coaches was a guy by the name of Ron James, who I enjoyed working

YOUR DECISIONS DETERMINE YOUR DESTINY

with. I believe that the decision was already made (by God) before we formally went through the motions. I took a position as a *Life Coach* that seemed to fit perfectly to the areas in which I am strong. Many of my friends that knew me well commented, "That will a perfect fit for you." More of God's confirmation.

After being there for my first month, I decided to trade my car in for a later model Cadillac, which incidentally is my third one. I seem to have developed a preference for that type of automobile. At the dealership, I made a call to my wife to get her input on this decision because I realize and respect the fact that any major financial purchases that will affect our home, I need to welcome her input. I explained some of the details of the deal over the phone and she told me to go for it. Around that same first month on this job, I experienced a very serious flare up with my ulcerated colitis, continually. Question is, *how bad do you really want this* position? I'm talking to client's one on one and at times I immediately have to get up and run to the bathroom, most of the time I did make it safely. A few of the times, I did not. I informed my supervisor what I was going through and so that he could clearly see my struggle and the challenge for me to remain in this position. A couple times, I had to actually go home to take a shower and change my clothes. I believe it was more of a psychological torture than anything else. I prayed and I prayed for God to show me which direction to take because I strongly believed that I *could not* continue with that type of medical issue in a counseling environment. I seriously considered quitting this job that myself and many others strongly felt was perfect for me. *How bad do you want it?*

I kept leaning on my G.I. doctor for relief and reliable control. He was doing the best he could and assured me that my process will improve. After a couple of different combinations of medication, he finally stabilized me where I could have a peace of mind and not constantly be in fear of having those accidents and very strong *urges to go*. I had to even try those Depends for a couple of days, which were so uncomfortable and so embarrassing. At the time, that was my reality and you either embrace your reality or you pay the consequence for being in denial. That question continues to challenge me, *How bad do you*

How Bad Do You Want It?

want it? I finally realized that from a spiritual perspective, I apparently was about to play a significant role in uplifting and empowering many people. I seriously believe that I was under a spiritual attack to be deterred from functioning in that capacity. In other words, the whole thing was bigger than me.

I made the decision to remain despite the immediate challenges I had to persevere through and I was so glad that I did. After working in this position for over two years I've come to recognize the fact that a life coach is not what I do, but who I am. And I say this with sincerest humility and accurate acknowledgement of what Almighty God designed for me to do. I always struggled with firmly acknowledging my strengths out of concern what others may think. Not anymore. All employees of this organization are required to do a fingerprint and FBI background check. Uh oh! This was required for me to do after a year into my employment.

Out of fear and wisdom, I was compelled to pull my supervisor to the side one day during the first week of my employment. I informed him that when I was in my addiction, I had to seriously hurt this guy to keep him from shooting me. I was scared for my life and everything happened so fast. I told my supervisor that I caught an Attempted Murder charge and did some time for it. I just want to let you know just in case in comes up later. He told me that back in the day, he used to be a *gang banger*, and I was relieved.

My FBI report came back to my home and when I opened the letter, my jar almost dropped to the floor. Yes, I had forgotten about many lightweight charges I have accrued over the years, but the way they worded the big one, I thought was truly unnecessary. It read at the top of the front page in thick bold letters: MURDER: FIRST DEGREE-ATTEMPTED. My first reaction was "Got Damn," and then my second reaction was why they didn't put the *attempted* in front instead of the rear, scaring me to death like that. I quickly ran around to the job to explain. I happened to run into the vice president of the company in the parking lot. When I showed her the FBI report her eyes bulged out a little bit. I then said, "Let me explain," and I did.

YOUR DECISIONS DETERMINE YOUR DESTINY

She then put her hand on my shoulder and assuringly said "Steve"; we're not letting you go." I was so relieved. To me this is not just a profession, but also an assignment. I work alongside a strong team and the leadership is truly filled with and led by the spirit of God. I can honestly say that I not only love what I do, but I also love the team I'm assigned to. Although the players change from time to time, it is truly God engineered.

One thing I love more than anything else is uplifting people and getting them to see themselves through a better perspective. Helping them to realize that their current situations and circumstances do not by any means reveal the hidden potential deep inside of them that's waiting to be released. I have a NA sponsor by the name of Terry H. Over a significant number of years, we have cultivated a very close relationship and he has been very instrumental in pushing me toward my destiny. I myself sponsor so many strong men and it continues to humble me how God allows me to have an impact on so many. Since I subscribe to the work ethic of *always do more than what you're getting paid to do*, I began teaching a class on *Spiritual Warfare* and a class on a *12 Step Spiritual Journey*.

The feedback that I constantly get is truly amazing and very encouraging. Communication of information is one of my strong points and I accomplish this gift in a number of ways. I realized that I had the *gift of gab* when I was on the streets doing wrong, now I use this gift to help motivate those of us that need a little push. Only by the grace of God, I'm asked to speak at many functions, (some for a fee), and share a word of encouragement. Along with my good friend and partner Ron James, I have spoken to middle schools, high schools, have been the keynote speaker at college graduating ceremonies, and just recently played a small part as a convict in the movie *Choices*, the life story of Ron James, a repeated offender. I go out of town on occasions to do *Crises Interventions* with troubled families.

This one project is where a young man was struggling with his drug addiction and his family was very concerned. When I arrived there, I was greeted by this young man's uncle and his wife. The mom and his stepfather were there, his real father was there, and grandma and

How Bad Do You Want It?

granddad were there also. He arrived about a half an hour later after I had a chance to establish a different perspective and attempt to carve a new path of action. It didn't go as well as I would have liked, however, the information I shared was worth the fee I charged and eventually the young man placed himself in a long-term treatment facility. Through partnership, I continue to do crises interventions as well as private life coaching projects. I particularly enjoy when our team travels to New York or New Jersey to speak on right choices to the so-called *at risk* young teenagers. What we advocate is that they're at risk all right, *at risk for success*. When you can change someone's perspective, you change the way they see things thus giving them more options.

I have learned through life that some things that are revealed at a particular moment in time, is like a *time release capsule*, later on the effect will take hold. Through my various videos and my first book, *Life Love Liberty* where I illustrate a composite of poems that almost everyone that I know, can relate to, identify with and be encouraged from deep within. It's not where you came from, but where you are going, and most importantly, what you learn along the way. Any and all decisions must be carefully thought out, assuming that the desired end is a good result. True, some decisions do not require careful deliberation, however, those decisions that affect your road to your destiny will. By God's grace, I continue to function and operate in the capacity that I was already predestined to do. It took a great many years to finally get to a designated place and be confident while being there. Now in my mid-sixties, I feel that life has taken on a whole new meaning. I still believe that the best is yet to come. As Tony Evans so profoundly describes it, "It's a reason why my windshield is much bigger than my rearview mirror. What's in front of me is much larger and greater than what is behind me. That's where all my focus, energy, and concentration should be on, what lies ahead."

"I can't go back and create a new beginning; however, from this point forward, I can create a new ending." Almost all of my decisions that I have made throughout my lifetime help to shape, mold, and guide my path, many times without my awareness. I'm still very much amazed and in awe, after all the mess and close calls I've came through, destiny was waiting for me. My destiny is not coming, it's already here.

Conclusion/ Summary

―――⟫•◆•⟪―――

Pausing at any period of your life eventually requires a decision to keep moving forward. If and when I may find myself being stuck, I need to make a decision to move forward or I unknowingly just made the decision to remain there. As I see how certain decisions throughout my life helped shape and determine where I'm at in the present, the importance of making good decisions becomes more apparent. Even way back in time as a young boy, I was attracted to strong guys in the movies with muscles, such as Hercules and Samson. Right there at that point in time, I decided as a kid that was the way I wanted to be and look. Not realizing the deep influence of that particular decision would stamp into my subconscious an image that would reveal itself much later down the road and even into my adult life. And how about being a follower with the crowd, despite the consequences and the price that I would pay as a result. Deciding to give into peer pressure only because I wanted to be accepted and that I put too much stock in what others say or think about me. Falling into that peer pressure only revealed a deeper issue

YOUR DECISIONS DETERMINE YOUR DESTINY

down to my core, which was clearly a low self-image. That led me to hook school, pick up that first drink and drug, and take on that rebellious and defiant posture which was indicative of my immediate surroundings and reflective of the times at hand.

Making the decision to join the US Army, (after the tradition of my father and brother who were both drafted), was by far one of the smartest decisions I could have made at the age of 17 years old. It not only exposed me to things that I would have never experienced otherwise, but it also opened several doors for me as a result of my veteran status. I'm sure that we all would agree that making decisions from desperation, drug induced pressure, or just very low self-esteem would easily result in regret or too high a cost to pay.

On the other hand, making decisions from that quiet, still voice from deep within your spirit can be very rewarding. Like one of the greatest decisions I made was to marry my wife Cherry. This woman is such a blessing to me that I constantly and sincerely thank God for her each and every day of my life. She naturally enhances me and brings to the table such a beautiful spirit that completes me in ways I could have never imagined. The decision to buy our home with all the responsibilities that came along with it was still the best way to go. Giving drug dealers, so much of my money over the years and enhancing *their* quality of life was a clear lesson for me not to repeat with a *landlord*. Going back to school in my late 50's although was initially motivated by greed, however, that decision proved to me instrumental for the next phase in my life. The nagging and unavoidable question of why I was put here on this earth, demanded a deep journey within and once discovered, making a conscious decision to cultivate and develop that purpose.

I began to realize that I was already a *life coach* before I assumed it as a profession. Having accumulated a vast source of information over the years, with a strong desire to learn, having the ability to articulate such information coupled with a burning passion to make a difference, have brought me to the realization that I am here to not only communicate information, but also do it with a meaningful passion. Being indecisive also keeps your foot on the brake pedal making it difficult, if not impossible,

Conclusion/Summary

to move forward to the next phase in your life. I have also come to learn that an impulsive decision based on temporary emotions tends to produce an unwanted outcome, because emotions and feelings change. Some of the very serious decisions need to be carefully deliberated on especially when the outcome of that decision effect many people. Various factors need to be considered and you may wisely have to allow other qualifying individuals to weigh in on that decision. Reaching out for help is not a weakness but a strength instead, because by getting different point of views, you have a broader perspective of the situation leaving you with different options to choose from. "How can you see the whole picture when you're standing in the frame?"

The quality of life that one will have generally rests upon the results of the decisions that you make. The quality of life that I would enjoy today is only a residual end of some decisions that I made or failed to make prior to this day showing up. So then, if that is the case, then the quality of life that I would have later is predicated on the decisions that I will make today. Naturally, not all decisions are that serious therefore not requiring a complicated process to arrive at. Some decisions such as what shirt I want to wear today have little significance in the bigger scheme of things. When I ultimately exhaust all my efforts of trying to control and manipulate the various aspects of my life, and make the decision to allow God to reveal His plan for me, then I have made the best decision that I could ever make in my entire life. Looking back, the accumulative and consistent decisions I have made over many years, although at times not having a clue, ultimately pointed me towards, and prepared me for the destination that awaited my arrival.

I thank Almighty God for graciously allowing me to participate in my journey keeping in mind a very clear conclusion, "It's not where you've been, but the real purpose of you being there and the *vehicle* that was being formed to carry you to your destiny."